Values and
humanity

Values and humanity

ELIZABETH MONROE DREWS
AND LESLIE LIPSON

St. Martin's Press   New York

AFFILIATED PUBLISHERS
Macmillan & Company, Limited, London—also at Bombay, Calcutta, Madras
and Melbourne; The Macmillan Company of Canada, Limited, Toronto.

To the memory of Abraham H. Maslow

Preface

In recent years, the age-old question of how we can rise to higher levels of civilization and consciousness has been reformulated in a more stark and urgent context. Mankind has grown aware of the real possibility that our species could destroy itself along with other forms of life on this planet. Yet simultaneously, we are recognizing that everyone has great potentialities which we have scarcely begun to realize. Whether we shall survive or not, and, if we do, whether we shall move into a new stage of development, depends on our own decisions which in turn depend on what we value most.

The two of us who co-authored this book have come by different routes to similar conclusions. One of us has studied the inner world of psychology. Elizabeth Drews is a psychologist who first majored in Art and is now on the Faculty of a School of Education. She found the possibilities for developing new programs, for helping students to discover their more imaginative and creative selves, better in Education than they were in Psychology, particularly in its academic form. The other has studied the outer world of politics. Leslie Lipson is a political scientist whose intellectual roots are in classical history and literature as well as in philosophy. He remains profoundly sceptical of the appropriateness of the term science in the title of his discipline.

If asked to describe ourselves, however, we would both prefer to say that, first and foremost, we are humanists and generalists. We are more concerned with the present and with what lies ahead, than with the past. We hold that our species is unique; that human nature, as Rousseau held, is basically good; that all aspects of humanity have to be viewed as a whole; and that our human characteristics can never be fully understood by analogies with systems, with the technology of machines, or the behavior of rats and guinea-pigs. Moreover, since knowledge is subjective to a large extent, we consider the notion of a purely objective, value-free science both false and illusory. Values are central to living; they are inseparable from understanding. That being so, we must face our values explicitly, choose them knowingly, and make very certain that our choices are the higher, more human, ones. Knowing that we are free to choose, we must be aware that our decisions could diminish or enlarge our world and ourselves. If we choose well, there are no limits to the transformations which can result.

In this book, we are concerned with the values of the individual who seeks not only to realize his or her potential as a unique person, but at the same time to unite with others in a network of communities from small to universal. The uniqueness and the universality are equally important aspects of human existence. The former can be expressed through self-affirmation; and the latter through the ethic of social service.

A new world is in the making and is being brought about by new kinds of people. If our contemporary culture is in convulsions, this is because it incorporates opposing values and thus exhibits some glaring contradictions. In certain senses, we are becoming more moral, more humane. But the demands of material acquisition and technological change have been imposing other behavior-patterns which are less moral or even outright immoral. Ahead of us are many avenues of development, including two alternatives which are clear-cut and sharply contrasted. We could enter a wholly technocratic society where the machines will run the people. Already we have had a taste of what life can be like when we are at the beck and call of technology and the market. And theoretically a programmed, cybernated, computerized future is a possibility. In reality, however, it is not apt to occur. Human beings will resist. In fact, the present widespread unrest indicates that people will not tolerate such a domination. The alternative could be a new age of humanity, where our species would live at peace with itself and in harmony with the natural environment. This would be a truly revolutionary occurrence. To some, it will sound utopian, in the sense of visionary. We contemplate it in all seriousness, however, because in this increasingly perilous world, such utopian thought is the truest realism.

We offer this book to our readers, not as one more academic exercise, but as a way to help you think about your personal life styles and the philosophies on which these are based. The failings of our contemporary society have been trenchantly exposed and abundantly documented in many current works. But our feeling was that there is a need to consider positive directions. Affirmation is more necessary than criticism. We cannot change unless we see an avenue to take. If there is much that is wrong with our present priorities, by what values should our future choices be guided?

In our judgment, humanity will progress by removing boundaries (within our heads as well as outside), by demanding of science, industry, and government that they serve the higher human values (not consumption, power and status), and by combining experience with experiment. It is well to realize that there are no endings, no beginnings. Rather, there is a continuity of learning, change, and growth. Some of our older values are being rediscovered. New ways of putting them into practice are being explored. Many of these are not the result of systematic thought, in the narrow sense, but of a higher reason. And much of the change has come from youth, particularly those who are called forerunners. The world is too dangerous for despair—and already there are stirrings around us which justify genuine hope.

In formulating and developing this philosophy, both of us owe a tremendous debt to that inspiring scholar, the late Abraham H. Maslow, to whose memory we have dedicated our book. A man of vision, a humanist, an eminent psychologist, and a distinguished generalist, he found time for over a decade for many interviews and conversations with Elizabeth Drews when she was trying to develop guidelines for a more personal and human education. Particularly, he encouraged her to write. And when he moved to the West Coast in 1969 he shared several precious days with both of us discussing the problems of values. The stimulus of his suggestions will be readily apparent to the reader in the chapters that follow.

To two other friends, we are also indebted. Willis Harman, Director of the Educational Policy Research Center, Stanford Research

Institute, requested Elizabeth Drews to prepare the original study, on which she consulted with Leslie Lipson and which has been revised and expanded to form the present book. Her report was published in 1970 under the title *Policy Implications of a Hierarchy of Values* (EPRC Research Memorandum 6747-8, Stanford Research Institute). We are grateful to Dr. Harman for his insights into present trends and future possibilities, his searching and constructive comments, and his generous help at all stages of this project.

Finally, the sociologist, Henry Anderson, of the State Department of Public Health, Berkeley, California, undertook a chore which is the sign of true friendship and concern. He not only read this book in manuscript form, but offered us pages of informed and challenging criticism. We should like to thank him for helping us to improve a number of specific passages, and for sharing with us his illuminating perception of the general philosophy of values.

Contents

In the affairs of men there is a system.
LAO TZU

*Marvels are many and none is more
marvelous than Man.*
SOPHOCLES

*Things are ever grouping themselves to
higher and more interior laws.*
RALPH WALDO EMERSON

*There is a way of thinking which destroys
and a way which saves.*
GILBERT MURRAY

Introduction

This is an inquiry into values, into their source and meaning, and their relation and relevance to humanity. In the deepest sense, the inquiry is about the qualities which make us human. "What a piece of work is man!" was Shakespeare's admiring comment on our species. But what is the nature of man? That is the perennial question which reflective people have asked anew in every generation. The answer we are suggesting is this: As human beings, we are what we value. It is by our values, our philosophy of life, that we recognize and discover ourselves. Through these we become enlightened.

We are distinguished from all living species by the fact that we are both aware of what we are and can aspire to be something more. A human being is a creature of the present with a memory of the past and a vision of the future. In retaining this memory, in possessing that vision, and in communicating with fellow-humans, we are living a life of the mind. This we do through symbols, such as language, and an unlimited variety of other means. Not only are we self-aware, but within each of us is the capacity to create our own destiny. This we do by the choices we make, both conscious and unconscious. For we are value-selecting animals. That is to say, we strive for goals which have value for us. Anything we do or fail to do involves affirmation or rejection, a preference for this over that.

All people hold certain things to be above others. For example, we prefer to live than to die, to be fed than to starve, to be treated kindly instead of cruelly, to see beauty rather than ugliness. Under special conditions, of course, some of these priorities may be temporarily reversed. One may go without eating, even when hungry, in order to search for truth, to revel in beauty, or to experience love. If we spend a considerable portion of our time watching television, so much less of it will be left for reading or writing a book, for nursing the sick or teaching the ignorant. Whoever is a hard-driving, aggressive, ruthless person may sometimes obtain certain results for himself by outwitting or vanquishing others. He may show himself their superior in strength or shrewdness, and may thereby win the laurels or take the spoils. He may also, in these efforts to command others by instilling fear, reduce them to apathy. However, in this process he will doubtless forfeit their esteem—and most certainly he will not be loved. So he must make a choice, which will be influenced by his conceptions of what values he holds higher. These are what the psychologist Abraham H. Maslow has called "a natural value system, a court of ultimate appeal for the determination of good and bad, or right and wrong."[1] As the psychoanalyst Erich Fromm stated: "Values are rooted in the very conditions of human existence; hence . . . our knowledge of these conditions, that is, of the human situation, leads us to establishing values which have objective validity. . . ."[2]

It follows from this that values have to be ranked in a hierarchy. When different values compete for fulfillment, the necessity of choosing implies a judgment that what is preferred is better than what is rejected. Without a hierarchy, therefore, no meaning would attach to the choice. Indeed, in the larger sense, no meaning would attach to life itself. If nothing is thought of as better than anything else, how can a person know which way to grow? How does one determine which direction is up and which is down? The individual who does not consciously formulate a hierarchy and seek to live by it does not, by such behavior, rule it out of account. One aspect of our behavior about which we have no choice at all is that we must, and do, make choices continually. Indeed, to live is itself to choose. But what is crucial is whether we are aware that this is so and consciously confront the responsibility of choosing, or whether we lack this awareness. In the latter case, we may doom ourselves to mill and muddle, to live capriciously and without clarity of purpose and to be unlikely to develop the best that is in us. Only in the former case, when we avow our preferences and make conscious choices, can we call ourselves free.

The whole point in existence is to flourish as a human being. This requires a person to think about what it means to be human in the fullest, most developed sense. Since changes are constantly occurring in the development both of the individual and of society, without a philosophy of life one could not distinguish in any significant way between the kind of growth which is improvement and that which is merely accretion, between the better and the different. A hierarchy of values is needed, therefore, because it endows human life with a standard for decision-making, a rationale and a goal.

Values, as is already evident, have many connotations. All values, as Aristotle stressed, are what humanity—or some humans—conceive to be good. But goodness, in and by itself, is only an abstract form unless it has a content. What is called good may be the beauty of nature, an act of compassion, a statement of truth, the courage of a person of integrity, the physical and psychic energy of a healthy person, and so on. This means that the good is always envisioned in different forms—as truth for example, or as beauty, as justice or love —which may be differently ranked. Not only must a value be valuable to somebody, but it must also be attached to something—and this attachment can assume many guises. One may value a person (a saint) or a relationship with a person (one's beloved); a thing (a hi-fi set) or a relationship with a thing (experiencing a sunrise); or an ethical ideal (justice) or some blend of abstract ideas and concrete institutions (world government).

A hierarchical ordering of values can be applied, as will be shown later, to the individual (in the ideal form of the Good Person) as well as to the community (in the ideal form of the Good Society). In addition, one may apply similar priorities to knowledge. It is more important to learn some things than others, but the most important of all is to arrive at a philosophy for guiding one's life. We find this guidance not only by becoming attuned to our inner selves, but also by discovering models to learn from and emulate. In his concept of "superior knowledge," the physicist Michael Polanyi suggested that we should search the classics for guidelines and look to what "heroes and saints have done."[3] Plato saw that to develop values was essential for the Good Person and the Good Society. That was why in the curriculum for his philosopher-kings philosophy was placed at the pinnacle.[4] Matthew Arnold believed that one route for reaching such understandings of self and of life was poetry. It was his view that poetry should serve an ethical purpose, be "a criticism of life," tell us "how to live." The point is that to be more fully human we must be exposed to the best that has been thought and said.[5] As this happens, as our imagination becomes "educated,"[6] our very thoughts—and with them our life style—will change.

If we are to say, then, with Alexander Pope that "the proper study of mankind is man," we shall only understand what constitutes our humanness by an examination of what we prize and what we spurn. That which differentiates humanity from the other animals is certainly not our sense organs or bodily powers—for in each of these the human being is inferior to some other creature. Where we excel them is in our capacities for thought and imagination. These are what enable us to endow our daily activities with meaning, to lead lives which are imbued with purpose. It is not necessary that we lead meaningless lives. Through our imaginative powers, we can celebrate the glories of the past and contemplate a utopian future. Because we are human, we can evaluate and select, decide and plan. And, as we do this, values—conscious or unconscious, explicit or implicit, central or peripheral—will be present. Wherever there are human beings, there are accompanying values; where values are, there you will find humanity.

In describing ourselves, therefore, as value-selecting animals, and in saying that our values have to be ranked in a hierarchy, we are arguing that three characteristics are fundamental to humanity: the need to choose, our subjective awareness that we are choosing, and our need to choose well. It is not the act of choosing alone which suffices, since there are many who choose badly. Genghis Khan, Adolf Hitler made their deliberate choices and they assuredly valued what they chose. So, too, did Gautama, Socrates and Jesus. Between such extremes lie millions of choices which extend along a continuum from evil to good. Moreover, toward the center there are all those whose lives consist more of avoidances than affirmations. They do not steal, nor do they give to others. They refrain from murder, but do not try to stop wars. So complex is human nature that there have been advocates and practitioners of evil through passivity, as well as of good. It is because the priority should be given to the good —to truth, beauty, and love—that how we arrange our values becomes so important. That is why it is necessary to discuss what we should value if we are to become more fully human.

CHAPTER ONE

Five images of man

It is characteristic of all of us to develop images of ourselves and of
our relation to the world around us. For humanity is distinguished
from other living species by the fact of self-consciousness. Being
aware that we exist, we know that this awareness endows our lives
with significance. To understand what this significance may be, we
paint a self-portrait or take our own picture. We are, in other words,
acting on the advice of the Delphic oracle that we should know ourselves. The manner in which we do this is typically human, for in
thought and imagination we construct images which serve as symbolic representations. It is by these that we seek to portray what we
believe not only ourselves but our species to be like. Some images
are monochromatic, some impressionistic; but many are done with
the full palette or with the explicit realism of the candid camera.
Every image is a collection of the choices or values which we use as
a basis for self-evaluation, sitting in judgment on ourselves. Because
there are many styles and colors to choose from, and a multitude of
choosers, the images vary. Some, however, stand out as particularly
vivid and have been repeated enough to be the expressions of a dis-
tinctive school of thought. Of these, five will be referred to here,

because they are strikingly drawn and have recurred throughout history.

Homo homini lupus—man is a wolf to his fellowmen

According to the most pessimistic view, man is an antisocial, aggressive and immoral creature whose behavior is stimulated by ever-dangerous instincts. This is an image in western thought which is at least as old as the Greeks. Both the historian Thucydides and the philosopher Plato allowed its spokesmen to express it in their writings. The former narrates how the Athenians demanded the submission of the islanders of Melos on the ground that the security of their naval empire required it and that the strong are entitled to do whatever they think will benefit them.[7] Similarly, Plato puts in the mouth of the sophist, Thrasymachus, the unequivocal assertion that justice is the interest of the stronger.[8]

The unflattering image of humanity as basically evil and destructive received some of its most uncompromising portrayals amid the revolutionary turbulence of the 16th and 17th centuries. This, for instance, is how Machiavelli sees humankind in one passage of *The Prince*: "For it may be said of men in general that they are ungrateful, voluble, dissemblers, anxious to avoid danger, and covetous of gain. . . . Men forget more easily the death of their father than the loss of the patrimony."[9] Likewise, Calvin brings against all mankind an indictment for sin which he dates from the time of birth:

"Infants themselves, as they bring their condemnation into the world with them, are rendered liable to punishment by their own sinfulness, not by the sinfulness of another. For though they have not yet produced the fruits of their iniquity, yet they have the seed of it within them; even their whole nature is as it were a seed of sin."[10]

Similar in mood is Hobbes, who employs psychology rather than theology to construct a political philosophy which is grimly pessimistic. In *Leviathan* we read:

"So that in the first place, I put for a generall inclination of all mankind a perpetuall and restlesse desire of power after power, that ceaseth only in Death. And the cause of this, is not alwayes that a man hopes for a more intensive delight, than he has already attained to; or that he cannot be content with a moderate

Hereby it is manifest, that during the time men
live without a common Power to keep them all in awe,
they are in that condition which is called Warre;
and such a Warre, as is of every man, against every
man. . . . In such condition . . . continuall feare,
and danger of violent death; And the life of man,
solitary, poore, nasty, brutish, and short.

This passage from Hobbes (Leviathan, Chapter XIII)
is illustrated by Boris Pasternak's account of some
of the events that accompanied the Bolshevik
Revolution and the subsequent Civil War between
Reds and Whites.

That period (he writes), confirmed the ancient
proverb, "Man is a wolf to man." Traveller turned
off the road at the sight of traveller, stranger
meeting stranger killed for fear of being killed. There
were isolated cases of cannibalism. The laws of
human civilization were suspended. The jungle law
was in force. Man dreamed the prehistoric dreams of
the cave dweller.

(Doctor Zhivago, trans. by Max Hayward and Manya Harari;
New York: Pantheon Books, Inc., 1958, p. 378.)

---

power: but because he cannot assure the power and the means to
live well, which he hath present, without the acquisition of more."[11]

As thus portrayed, man is completely egotistic. He is concerned primarily with his own interests and security. Towards others he is aggressive and predatory, seeking to subordinate them to his will and thereby eliminate any threat to himself. Again in Hobbes' own words: "Competition of Riches, Honour, Command, or other power, enclineth to Contention, Enmity, and War: Because the way of one Competitor, to the attaining of his desire, is to kill, subdue, supplant, or repell the other."[12] But if all were left free to act in this manner, the net result would be mutually destructive anarchy, the war of every man against every man which Hobbes describes. If that is not to happen, and if men are to coexist even minimally, they must be conditioned, restrained, and overawed. Institutions must be so organized as to curb the evil inherent in human nature and minimize the savagery of which we are capable. Even these, however, cannot escape the taint which they are designed to control, because good institutions cannot emanate from men who are bad. Hobbes' conclusions exactly illustrate this reasoning. The logical consequence of his psychological assumptions is Leviathan, the power of the state—that "mortal God," as he calls it. The essence of Leviathan is its omnipotence. Only their fear of it will force men to coexist in a semblance of order.

Down to modern times the pessimistic picture has continued to have strong proponents. In the 19th century, one of the more notable, or notorious, misanthropes was Schopenhauer, who envisaged his fellowmen as analogous to porcupines. Is it possible for such creatures to coexist sociably? His answer was this parable:

> "A company of porcupines crowded themselves very close together one cold winter's day so as to profit by one another's warmth and so save themselves from being frozen to death. But soon they felt one another's quills, which induced them to separate again. And now, when the need for warmth brought them nearer together again, the second evil arose once more. So that they were driven backwards and forwards from one trouble to the other, until they had discovered a mean distance at which they could most tolerably exist."[13]

It is highly significant that Schopenhauer's parable of the porcupines was cited by Freud in his work on *Group Psychology and the Analysis of the Ego,* for the founder of psychoanalysis was himself a powerful contributor to the notion that human beings are bad animals. Indeed, his portrait of mankind is almost as unflattering as those painted by Machiavelli and Hobbes. "The bit of truth behind all this—one so eagerly denied—is that men are not gentle, friendly creatures wishing for love. . . . Hatred is at the bottom of all the relations of affection and love between human beings."[14] Such a statement justifies Karen Horney, the psychoanalyst, in this summation of the Freudian image of human nature: "Freud left no doubt about its meaning: man has an innate drive toward evil, aggressiveness, destructiveness, cruelty."[15] Not surprisingly, therefore, Maslow, the principal founder of modern humanistic psychology, has commented that "it is as if Freud supplied to us the sick half of psychology."[16]

The response of the oracle of Vienna to the oracle of Delphi supplies much food for reflection in view of the tremendous influence which Freud has wielded in the 20th century. What for him were hypotheses, biases, or intuitions, have not only become the clichés of many an academic department, but they have spread to the stage, the canvas and the popular media. Nor was this doom-laden analysis unaided by the actual deeds of such men as Hitler and Stalin. For what bad animals were ever worse than those?

Tabula rasa—man is a blank sheet, receiving external impressions

A second image portrays humanity as amoral and our nature, at bottom, as ethically neutral. This view follows from the psychological doctrine advanced by John Locke in his *Essay on the Human Understanding*. Human beings at birth are regarded as blank sheets. Whatever is printed on us is solely the result of subsequent external stimuli which are relayed to the mind by sense perceptions. Locke, who was greatly impressed by Newton's mechanistic view of the universe, stated his basic principle thus:

> "Let us then suppose the mind to be, as we say, white paper, void of all characters, without any ideas; how comes it to be furnished? Whence comes it by that vast store, which the busy and boundless fancy of man has painted on it with an almost endless variety? Whence has it all the materials of reason and knowledge? To this I answer in one word, from EXPERIENCE; in that all our knowledge is founded, and from that it ultimately derives itself."[17]

The Lockean hypothesis that all our ideas are implanted in us after birth and that none are innate has lent itself in the 20th century to a far-reaching extension with dangerous implications. The scientific basis for this extension was provided by the work of the Russian physiologist, Pavlov, who generalized the results of his experiments in the concept of the conditioned reflex—according to which a person can be conditioned (trained) to respond to a given stimulus in a predetermined fashion. If so, is not the way open for some individuals to prescribe and then program what kind of conditioning others shall receive? J. B. Watson, the American psychologist, and his behaviorist school were not slow at seeing the possibilities or restrained in expressing them. In Watson's view, a human being is simply "an assembled organic machine ready to run." Consequently, as he saw it, "the possibility of shaping in any direction is almost endless."[18] The ultimate possibility we owe to another psychologist, B. F. Skinner, who has devised techniques for what is called "operant conditioning." His promise is that, when these are executed completely as designed, the result is a living organism—we would no longer say "human being"—that functions faithfully in response to stimuli which are externally administered. Everything depends, therefore, on who programs the machine, or, to revert to the other metaphor, writes on the *tabula rasa*. A piece of paper, like a computer, is neither good nor bad. Good or bad is what is written on it or fed into it. Since Lockean man is the creature of his environment, if that is good his character will be molded for the good. If it is bad, so will he be.

The social and political consequences which can follow from the acceptance and application of this principle are indeed significant. It is important to emphasize that this image of mankind as initially a collection of blank sheets would allow theoretically for alternative lines of development toward either good or evil. In fairness to Locke and his latter-day followers, one should recognize that none of these wished evil or intended it. Skinner himself in *Walden Two* has imagined a fully controlled environment which he considers a Utopia. But despite the intentions, evil in one form or another is virtually inherent in the doctrine.

Even if what is written on the sheet be good, it is still the writing of another and not the expression of oneself. The fully programmed "do-gooder" would still be merely an automaton ready to run, not an individual human being with an intrinsic conscience; a dehumanized thing, and not a person. In practice, however, the more probable result is that the writing or programming will be of the evil kind rather than the good. This is because the persons who write or program are assuredly going to be the powermongers, that is to say, those who are hungry for power and grasp the controls. Their primary concern is not so much the good of others as the maintenance of their own superiority, which requires that others remain subordinate. Thus the psychological theory of the *tabula rasa* fits in easily with the political practice of autocracy. These were the sinister conclusions which Aldous Huxley depicted in *Brave New World*. So did George Orwell in *1984*, where "Big Brother," omnipresent and omnipotent, emerges as the supreme conditioner. But there is no need to resort to fiction for such portrayals. One can readily see why such a political personality as Chairman Mao could find the behaviorists much to his liking. The man who rules seven hundred million persons has this to say: "The outstanding thing about China's people is that they are poor and blank. On a blank sheet of paper, free from any mark, the freshest and most beautiful characters can be written."[19]

Man is a mixture of good and evil

Human nature may also be conceived as a union of opposites held together in dynamic tension. These opposites are good and evil. Our conduct is then thought of as oscillating between the two poles of a divided nature. If both of the latter are equally authentic and actual parts of our being, humanity in this view could be described as schizoethic.

Throughout its long history, this image has been variously projected. Not a few religions have held that mankind is composed of two natures which are in eternal conflict. In ancient Persia, Zoroaster personified the opposing tendencies as Ormuzd and Ahriman. The former represented goodness and light; the latter symbolized evil and darkness. Within us lay the arena for their conflict. "It is the human soul," said Zoroaster, "in which the battle rages."[20] This fundamental dualism, which the Persians introduced into religion, was continued in Mithraism. To the same effect is the traditional notion in Christianity that God and Satan are two forces ever competing for the capture of the human soul. This ideal finds dramatic expression in the Faust legend, where a scholar is depicted as bartering his soul to the Devil in exchange for a few years of knowledge and power. "Two souls within me strive for the mastery," write Goethe in his latter-day version of the myth.

More recently, a similar characterization has received literary expression in terms which owe more to psychology than theology. Conan Doyle interpreted Dr. Jekyll and Mr. Hyde as the two manifestations of one personality, each incompatible with the other. This theme is also central to the *Steppenwolf* of Hermann Hesse, where it is presented as the tragedy of human society in the 20th century. In this case, the novelist depicts "the wolf from the steppes" as being in society, but at war with his fellowmen and with himself.

"And so the Steppenwolf had two natures, a human and a wolfish one. This was his fate. . . . In him the man and the wolf did not go the same way together, but were in continual and deadly enmity. . . . Now with our Steppenwolf it was so that in his conscious life he lived now as a wolf, now as a man, as indeed the case is with all mixed beings."[21]

What is uncertain about this analysis is the relation between cause and effect. Does the "schism in the soul," as Arnold Toynbee has phrased it, project outward and foment discord in the body politic, or do the contradictions within our social system reach inward and tear the psyche apart? What is also uncertain when humanity is so depicted is whether the conflict within the individual can be re-solved. Some appear to hold that it cannot. If good and evil are equally fundamental to our nature, granted the incompatibility, the duel between them cannot end. The forces of light and darkness remain in eternal combat, now one being uppermost and now the other; and the individual is held in thrall, doomed to be pulled this way and that, as was the fate of Steppenwolf. But the other possi-bility is that we human beings determine our own fate by the choices we make. We are therefore free either to save or to destroy our-selves. Faust suffered the consequences of having voluntarily entered into a compact with the devil, and Dr. Jekyll brought on his own destruction. In the religious view, however, people can reject evil and choose the good, thereby redeeming their souls. Such too is the opinion of Fromm, who interprets "the nature or essence of man [as] a contradiction which is rooted in the very conditions of human existence. This conflict in itself requires a solution, and basically there are only the regressive or progressive solutions."[22]

Man is naturally good and can improve himself

Another view is more optimistic. It envisages mankind—all human beings everywhere—as basically good and continuously improvable. All of us have goals and purposes which we formulate as good and strive to realize. If some of us are seen to be corrupted, this is be-cause the goodness intrinsic to our nature has been perverted by our social institutions. Once the latter are improved, we shall more readily exhibit the love, charity and cooperation which are funda-mental to us.

This image is the first of those we have considered which tilts the balance in favor of the good. It differs from the three preceding ones in expressing trust in mankind and voicing a hope for human betterment. Such an optimistic belief is both dynamic and developmental. It conceives of humanity, whether individually or as part of a community, in terms of growth which permits indefinite improvement. This outlook was prevalent among many philosophers of the 18th century—the Age of Enlightenment—and of the 19th, with its faith in progress. In fact, it accompanied or was used to justify the revolutions in the United States and France.

In France, Condorcet was a vigorous champion of the belief in mankind's natural goodness and in our capacity to become better than we are.[23] Likewise, Rousseau, in his earlier writings, contrasted the actual depravity of human beings with our potential goodness. "That men are actually wicked, a sad and continual experience of them proves beyond a doubt: But, all the same, I think I have shown that man is naturally good."[24] What has corrupted us, in Rousseau's view, is our institutions. Hence, if these can be drastically reconstructed, our natural goodness will assert itself.

In the United States, this faith is the common ground on which Paine and Jefferson took their stand. Paine's judgment was as follows: "As far as my experience in public extends, I have ever observed that the great mass of people are always just, both in their intentions and their object; but the true method of attaining such purpose does not always appear at once."[25] Jefferson argued similarly, basing his idea on the conviction that there is a moral sense implanted universally in all. "Man was destined for society," he wrote. "His morality, therefore, was to be formed to this object. He was endowed with a sense of right and wrong, merely relative to this. This sense is as much a part of his nature as the senses of hearing, seeing, and feeling. . . . State a moral case to a ploughman and a professor. The former will decide it as well, and often better than the latter, because he has not been led astray by artificial rules."[26] With such thinkers it was an article of faith that the use of intuitive reason (as expressed in the belief in self-evident truth) will lead humanity toward tolerance, sociability, and respect for others. Following them, a number of dedicated idealists and practical reformers —for example, Florence Nightingale, William Morris, N.F.S. Grundtvig, Leo Tolstoy, Jane Addams, Jacob Riis, Margaret Sanger, Mohandas Gandhi, and Albert Schweitzer—applied this notion directly in social experiments. Their aim was to design better institutions in which human goodness would find an outlet. Why, they ask, should not man put an end to his old antagonisms and base his society on love for his fellowman?

Both Freud and Adler . . . regard the infant as
"bad" by nature and as having to be made "good"
by external compulsion, or else allowed outlet
for its badness. I consider that the germ of goodness
or of love is in the individual (of every species
which has evolved a nurtured infancy) from the very
beginning, and that our traditional method of
upbringing frustrates this spontaneous benevolence
and substitutes "guilt-anxiety" morality for natural
goodness.

Ian D. Suttie, *The Origins of Love and Hate*, London: 1935,
p. 52.

Man will transcend himself

The last of the five images, as its name implies, transcends the rest.
Of the qualities which it imputes to mankind, some build upon the
usual ways of knowing and seeing; but others can only come from
forces as yet dimly defined and understood. Blake has made such
inferences, as have Emerson and the transcendentalists, and there is
more which the mystical religions of the Orient have contributed. In
Blake's words: "Man's perceptions are not bounded by organs of
perception; he perceives more than sense (tho' ever so acute) can
discover." "The desire of Man being Infinite, the possession is Infinite and himself Infinite." And again: "If the doors of perception
were cleansed every thing would appear to man as it is, infinite. For
man has closed himself up, till he sees all things thro' narrow chinks
of his cavern."[27]

For these insights, words and logical thinking are inadequate
channels. Human beings are believed to be endowed with potentialities beyond anything expressed or realized thus far. These are said
to originate in the dim forests of the past, in the deepest strata of
unconscious memory, and to be evolving toward an Infinite visible
only to the eye of imagination. Every individual, so viewed, is a
spring, a fountainhead, of unlimited possibilities. "You think me the
child of my circumstances," wrote Emerson. "I make my circumstances. . . . I—this thought which is called I—is the mould into

*We can certainly now assert that at least a reason-
able, theoretical, and empirical case has been made for
the presence within the human being of a tendency
toward, or need for growing in a direction that
can be summarized in general as self-actualization,
or psychological health, and specifically as growth
toward each and all of the sub-aspects of self-
actualization, i.e., he has within him a pressure
toward unity of personality, toward spontaneous
expressiveness, toward full individuality and identity,
toward seeing the truth rather than being blind,
toward being creative, toward being good and a lot
else.*

Maslow, *Toward a Psychology of Being*, New York:
Van Nostrand, 2nd edition, 1968, p. 155.

---

which the world is poured like melted wax." On this assumption, all
of us are indeed born free, free to grow toward a nature surpassing
any that was realized before. For a person's true existence lies in the
realm of spirit, idea, and imagination. "The Transcendentalist,"
Emerson affirms, "adopts the whole connection of spiritual doctine.
He believes in miracle, in the perpetual openness of the human mind
to new influx of light and power; he believes in inspiration, and in
ecstasy."[28]

Of the five images presented here, this one alone displays a sense
of joy, a mystical optimism. It expresses the faith that human growth
will and must continue, that we shall rise above ourselves as our
potentialities are realized. As Emerson said: "There is never a fin-
ished man."[29] Through this insight, the philosophy of transcendentalism is closely akin to the contemporary psychological doctrine of
self-actualization. Self-actualizing persons, as Maslow described
them, are those who move forward toward an integrated development of the moral, aesthetic, and intellectual sides of their natures.
As individuals, they seek enlightenment, liberation, a higher consciousness, but always return to the community, as did the Bodhissatva or Plato's philosopher-king, to serve and be one with their
fellowmen.

The same ideal, or something akin to it, is expressed by many of those who are repelled by the practices of today's society and who rebel against the imperatives which its system and its technology fasten upon the individual. They say with Emerson: "Nothing is at last sacred but the integrity of your own mind." Such works as Theodore Roszak's *The Making of a Counter Culture* or Charles A. Reich's *The Greening of America* voice the yearning for a new world—to be attained through a new consciousness of higher values. If there is a revolution abroad, it is a revolution of values. And, what else are the values it seeks but transcendental?

So different are these five images that one is bound to ask: Which, if any, is correct? The answer is of supreme importance because on it will hinge our attitude toward our fellowmen and much of our ensuing conduct. One of these images may in fact prove to be the correct one and may hold true for all persons without exception. But it is also conceivable that each of the five has its quota of representatives in the human race—in which case we could find examples of bad animals, of blank sheets receiving their imprint from others, of good and evil mixed, and of good in the ascendancy or even transcendent. Or again, is it not possible that some traits from each image may be present within every individual, but that the combination may vary in each of us and the resulting character types be differently balanced? Some may incline toward the transcendental or the good; others to the beast or the empty vessel. Moreover, the balance need not remain constant. It could possibly be alterable by circumstances—by a change in events or environment. Some of Hitler's erstwhile henchmen could become gentle nurses; the choirboy may graduate into the gangster.

Nor should it be overlooked that those who study human nature and formulate a general image must project a portion of themselves into the image they create or suggest. What an individual says about mankind at large cannot fail to reflect something of what the speaker is. In addition, judgments will be further influenced by the population sample one selects and studies. Freud was a doctor of medicine, who spent his life studying the psychologically ill, and who arrived at a jaundiced view of man. In contrast, Jung was a classical scholar who had read extensively in literary sources and, from concentrating on creative and autonomous people, judged that mankind has a limitless capacity for self-realization. Maslow, as a young psychologist, focused his interests on the Blackfoot Indians, and became concerned with synergy (the reciprocal effect of the good person and the good society). These led to his studies of human potentialities, including peak experiences—that is to say, the state which people attain when they are living to the fullest and are at the height of their powers. From this, he concluded that almost all human beings, unless hopelessly misdirected by bad education and other faulty socialization, can become self-aware and can transcend themselves.

Of these five images, the first two lie on the periphery of this inquiry, since they are not directly relevant to a hierarchy of values. The reason is that, when man is considered a bad animal or initially a blank sheet, nothing remains to be valued except power—in one case the power to avoid a violent death and survive unharmed, in the other the power to imprint what one wills on another. But when power is accepted as the arbiter of life, there is no other hierarchy than the measure of power. The greater power has the greater right. Such images of humanity are relativist, because they exclude any common standard of right. And they are also static, because they deny the possibility that we can improve ourselves.

Only when the image of mankind embraces the quality of goodness do considerations of values become relevant to human actions through the influence they exert upon motivations and goals. Hence, the last three of the images presented above are necessarily connected with the notion of a complex of values and of a hierarchy within that complex. These images are predicated on the idea that the individual can grow in positive ways. All of us, according to these concepts, have the capacity to become uniquely ourselves and also one with our fellowmen. All of us are influenced and, in some ways, shaped by externals; but, when we become self-aware, we are free to choose and are responsible for our choices. There is thus no limit, as Sartre has said, to our ability to transform ourselves. Such concepts, therefore, are dynamic. They permit the possibility of development in the direction of something better than already exists. They invite us to realize our potentialities to become, in a fuller measure, human.

CHAPTER TWO

The relation of values to actuality

Values—subject and object

What are values and what is their source? Why do people attach value to what they experience? Are values created or discovered or derived in some other way?

Such questions are fundamental in any consideration of values. The range of answers which have been proposed supplies an insight into a misleading intellectual habit with a long history—the habit of dividing our concepts into mutually exclusive alternatives. The result of this way of thinking is that, when you pick one alternative, you must reject the other. Truth must be Either-Or. It cannot be Both-And. The topic of values lends itself readily to the formulation of alternatives because one may so clearly distinguish two aspects of the act of valuing. There is the objective existence of whatever it is that is valued, as there is the subjective attitude or interest of the person to whom it is valuable.

Some thinkers have, accordingly, held that a value belongs to an object, or resides in a situation, and thence presents itself to the understanding. In that case, values exist quite independently of our wishing or feeling. An example of this view is the statement by the

19th-century British historian, J. A. Froude: "The eternal truths and rights of things exist, fortunately, independent of our thoughts or wishes, fixed as mathematics, inherent in the nature of man and the world. They are no more to be trifled with than gravitation."[30] To like effect, Thomas Carlyle asserted: "What have men to do with interests? There is a right way and a wrong way. That is all we need think about it."[31]

Others believe just the opposite—that value is wholly subjective, that it consists precisely of what we feel or wish. Consequently, when we say "this is good," what we mean is "I approve of this." Hobbes is a proponent of this doctrine and expresses it with his usual uncompromising clarity:

"But whatsoever is the object of any man's appetite or desire, that is it which he for his part calleth 'good;' and the object of his hate and aversions, 'evil;' and of his contempt 'vile' and 'inconsiderable.' For these words of good, evil, and contemptible, are ever used with relation to the person that useth them: there being nothing simply and absolutely so; nor any common rule of good and evil, to be taken from the nature of the objects themselves."[32]

During the last fifty years, this latter doctrine—that values have meaning only for those who express them—has been in vogue with many intellectuals, and among academicians in particular. It received a considerable impetus from the logical positivists, whose influence radiated outward from the Vienna School of the 1920s. Asserting that the value judgments of ethics and aesthetics are meaningless, they reduced these and all metaphysical topics to linguistics, to the analysis of verbal propositions. They affirmed that statements of "what is" are of a different order from statements of "what ought to be," and that the latter cannot be derived from the former. In fact, if one is a scientist, the question of "what ought to be" should not be investigated. Much of the study of human society which has been conducted in recent decades, as we shall discuss later,[33] has been influenced by the notion that it can and should be "value-free," because value judgments lack an objective basis. Such a notion, when pushed to the ultimate, is tersely reduced to this: "Value-judgments, Adieu!"[34]

The disagreement on whether values emerge from the facts of experience and, as it were, meet us in the eye, or whether personal feelings infuse our values into the facts, has run the customary course of arguments that hinge around two opposed alternatives. Fortunately, many insist that there is a third possibility. They see the subjective phenomenon of valuing and the objective existence of whatever is valued as interactive in a single process. This is the existentialist concept of being-in-the-world, a view which derives from the Danish theologian, Soren Kierkegaard. On this view, which is the one we hold, subjective values and objective facts interpenetrate one another and are a unity. As Emerson wrote, "the act of seeing and the thing seen, the seer and the spectacle, the subject and the object, are one."[35] Values, therefore, express both our conception of the world and its impact on us, taken together. The philosopher Samuel Alexander has put it this way:

> "In every value there are two sides, the subject of valuation and the object of value, and the value resides in the relation between the two, and does not exist apart from them."[36]

Essentially the same view was held by the *Gestalt* psychologist, Wolfgang Kohler. In his phrasing, "value and corresponding insight constitute the very essence of human mental life." A value, such as truth, "is a case of intrinsic requiredness" into which we succeed in obtaining insight—for example, when we say that "the situation cries out for remedy." Subject and object unite when you hear the cry.[37]

In this controversy, although many theorists cannot agree and are unable to reach a verdict, both history and the psychology of everyday life come to an agreement which is unmistakably clear. As we have seen, all of us develop values and live by them. These are formed, most often unconsciously, through experience and observation, and are used as a basis for the choices we make in the day-to-day business of living. Only the few who live "examined lives" in the Socratic sense are consciously aware of basic values, although these persons also act in accordance with values which are unconsciously held. But the point is that in every choice we make we inescapably express a value. Just as the conscious and the unconscious are inseparable parts of the whole, so are subject and object. Values are what integrate life and give it meaning.

How the subjective and objective are combined in the formulation of values, and how artificial are our boundaries, may be illustrated from the evolution of the concept and practice of liberty. In a specific situation (for example, in the American colonies between 1770 and 1776) people may complain about the unresponsive system which controls their lives. They then demand freedom from abuses A and B, and advocate positively the freedom to do C, D, and so on. These liberties, in the plural, they then generalize into the abstraction of Liberty. So conceived, Liberty is an extrapolation which goes far beyond the particulars. But once people become aware of the significance of Liberty, it will grow with a life of its own. As soon as any person or group has a vision of Liberty, it can become a reality for them. Eventually every barrier will fall before it.

Such, in fact, has been the history of some of the most famous formulations of basic human rights. The Magna Carta was drafted by the barons of England who mobilized their power to wring acquiescence from a reluctant king. The liberties in which these nobles were primarily interested were their own—and not those of their inferiors in the English feudal hierarchy. But fortunately for the future, the barons spelled out their rights in language so general that the application of Magna Carta was not restricted to their own small social class. Other Englishmen, therefore, could later invoke the same clauses for their own protection—eventually against the barons themselves. And by a still further extension, seven centuries later the descendants of these Englishmen, who in the meantime had amassed an empire, discovered that their non-English "subjects" were demanding similar liberties. Indians who studied at British universities could fortify their argument for independence with quotations from Magna Carta, as well as from John Milton and J. S. Mill.

The same has been true of the history of the Declaration of Independence. When Jefferson drafted his list of "self-evident truths," the first which he affirmed was "that all men are created equal." The emphatic word in that clause was "all." Its scope is universal. Every human being is included. There are no exceptions. Also, in stressing equality, Jefferson rejected the notion that there exist either submen or supermen. Humanity as such does not admit of grades or degrees. It consists of only one class—mankind, each member of which is like all others in being human. At the time when he wrote this, and when he and his colleagues signed the Declaration, neither he nor they expected the equality of "all men" to embrace all persons, whether female, poor, or black. Eventually, these extensions were granted in principle. The reality, however, continues to fall far short of genuine equality of opportunity or respect.

Education, like politics, can provide an example of how values have their roots in the relation between subject and object. Seven decades ago the philosopher John Dewey and his wife, Evelyn

Dewey, were launching the progressive education movement for the reform of the American schools. "There is an intimate and necessary relation," Dewey argued, "between the processes of actual experience and education." This view brought him into direct conflict with those traditionalists who saw education only as preparation for life, not as living itself.

Society in the United States is dedicated to the value of democracy. The general practices prevailing in the schools, however, were invariably authoritarian. The curriculum was formulated "from without" and imposed "from above." Education was "a process of overcoming natural inclination." Students were subjected to "straitjacket and chain-gang procedures," seated in "fixed rows of desks," and "permitted to move only at certain fixed signals." As a result of such "military regimen" they were to become "docile, receptive, obedient." They were, in effect, raw material to be molded and conditioned.[38]

Under such circumstances, Dewey asked, could they be expected to understand the meaning of freedom or of individuality, or of democracy itself? His remedy was clear and forthright: introduce democracy into the schools, welcome student participation, and understand each one's needs and growth pattern. In this way he hoped that democracy would become more than a principle to be voiced or a slogan to be fought for, and would be an experience which each had felt and sensed and lived. He always upheld the Emersonian dictum: The child must act it as life before he apprehends it as truth. For true understanding there must be an objective situation in which one has the subjective experience. As Dewey says, "If there is one conclusion to which human experience unmistakably points it is that democratic ends demand democratic methods for their realization."[39]

Values—the actual and the ideal

This sketch of the history of liberty and equality suggests another aspect of values which calls for comment: the relation of the actual to the ideal. In reading the history of the past and in our daily lives, we are continually making value judgments on concrete cases. Encountering a situation or a phenomenon, we evaluate it. (Here is a beautiful painting or an ugly building, a good mother or an unjust social system, a wise thinker or a poor argument.) Each of these terms, as Plato long ago insisted, implies an ideal criterion—beauty, justice, wisdom, etc. What is the relation between a value in a particular instance and its ideal extension?

An ideal, as we envisage it here, is a standard of perfection which our imagination projects far beyond any particular experience. It is the actual as it might be if it were purified and purged of imperfections. Of course, nothing real which exists measures up to the ideal or ever will. And to say that is not being cynical. Reality at its best can only consist of varying approximations of what our vision conceives at a particular moment. As Emerson observed, "We know better than we do." Moreover, the ideal itself is not fixed or static, but fluid and open. As we approach it in practice, we set new and better standards, for the ideal continues to evolve to still higher levels. A music critic reported that on one occasion he heard Arturo Toscanini, well-known for his perfection as an artist, conduct a rehearsal of a symphony by Mozart. At the end of this particular rendering which the critic judged as perfect, Toscanini put down his baton and merely said: "Thank you. We shall do better tomorrow."

The scope of every ideal is without limit; it is infinite. Valuing, therefore, is the complex process of applying a progressive standard to everchanging facts.

This principle is as apparent in the life of societies as in that of individuals. Reviewing American history, we can see that many of our social practices and numerous actions of our government have contradicted the ideals which this nation professes to uphold. Also, there is a further contradiction among the ideals themselves which represent contrasting levels of ethical attainment or, in Reich's view, stages of consciousness. (For further discussion, see Chapter IV on the stages of individual development.)

In the 19th century, except for the issue of slavery which was only resolved by civil war, there was a prevailing consensus—a common core of values of which most Americans were conscious and to which the majority subscribed. According to these, America was the land of opportunity where everybody had a fair chance to succeed in life, where the path to success was to practice the virtues of hard work, thrift, enterprise and competition, and where the measure of success was the acquisition of money. For two generations the McGuffey Readers reigned supreme and gave those who attended school a common foundation. Undoubtedly, this steady fare, with its strong doses of Protestant ethic, was a potent factor in molding the consciousness of our grandparents. Beyond this lay other stable structures. The home was hierarchical and all its members submitted to an authoritarian father as the final arbiter. Although in principle our form of government was considered a democracy, many tendencies to oligarchy persisted; and the democratic faith was further belied in the practices of many churches, schools and corporations.

But alongside the dominant American way, and no less authentically American, was a second route. The alternative had its source deep in the past, but it branched off from its European beginnings and transcended them. Its direction was toward the future, toward the light. This way was marked by the original values of our civilization, those of the Judeo-Christian ethic and, at a deeper and more mystical level, of what Leibniz and Aldous Huxley have called "the perennial philosophy." The life of the mind, the individual conscience, the higher consciousness—what Quakers mean by the "inner light" and Emerson by the "Over-Soul"—came to be celebrated by a group of New Englanders in a time (1830–60) which Lewis Mumford refers to as the Golden Age of the Mind.[40]

These Americans—Emerson, Thoreau and Whitman in particular —not only looked back into the past, but sought through their personal experiencing to develop the basis of a higher culture. This was to focus primarily on the unique worth of every individual. "Nothing," said Emerson, "is at last sacred but the integrity of your own mind." But the individual could attain his true humanity only by a universal communion with all life.

In American tradition, therefore, two sets of ideals are equally enshrined. The legends which we have erected around our heroes illustrate this. Franklin, Washington, Hamilton and John Adams have been placed in the Pantheon. But so, too, have Jefferson, Paine, Emerson and Thoreau. Understandably then, as later waves of immigration flowed to the American shore, the newcomers had a choice. The opportunity to participate in the dominant American Way was held out to Europeans who were invited before World War I to enter the melting pot where they would be fused into a common alloy. There were those, however, who rejected the values of a predominantly materialistic culture and defied its high priests. With Jefferson, they had glimpsed the vision of another America which was "the world's best hope." In the torch of Liberty's Statue they saw "a light that never was on sea or land."

But how can a people adhere to the maxim "To thine own self be true?" A dilemma is present in the philosophical values of democracy itself, whether this be the American version of it or any other.

One face of democracy looks to majority rule which is often identified with the general will, to the rightness of the greater number, and
to the supremacy of the law irrespective of its inherent justice or
injustice. But alongside of this, looking in a different direction, is the
other face which expresses concern for the individual and the
minority, which places rights above power and regards all people as
entitled to equal consideration within a context of social fluidity.
Democracy, so conceived, has been termed the first universal and
secular utopia. It may be thought of as patterned flux, in the form of
an open, upward, dynamic spiral.[41] This notion is in direct contrast
to concepts of unchanging absolutes, upheld by established authority. Adherence to fixed norms requires rigid interpretations of law
and undeviating rules which conflict with such fluidity.

The spontaneity and diversity of pluralism will always present a
challenge to any tendency to impose on society a uniform mold.
This challenge will be reflected not only in criticisms of social institutions but also in the questioning of conventional interpretations of
values, particularly when these are upheld and enforced by authority. Early in the 20th century the muckrakers, as they were then
called, strove to document the flaws in the prevailing society, stressing the gap between the actual and the ideal—a trend which was
carried forward strongly by the social critics of the thirties. The
ancient values enshrined in the Judeo-Christian ethic continued to
be intoned, as they still are. But the rulers of society and the average
citizens have been castigated in generation after generation for practices which depart from the precepts.

All of us, of course, are influenced by the structure of our society.
The requirements of order tend to shape everyone into a common
pattern; but the tension remains. The principles of a pluralistic
society continually invite diverse and autonomous growth. Democracy's problem is to combine its insistence on personal freedom with
a core of common understandings and shared values, so that each of
us may find our uniqueness respected and may also feel a sense of
community with other humans and with nature. The difference in
emphasis between these two conceptions becomes all-important
when the individual seeks to make a responsible moral judgment.
We cannot answer the question "What is going on here?" without
recognizing that each of us is part of a larger whole.[42]

Today, there is a renewed concern for morality and values which
has extended to many quarters. Education's new romantic critics,[43]
as well as the new theologians and many participants in the youth

revolution, raise many of the same questions. Youth in particular point to what they regard as the hypocrisy or blindness of the Establishment—in government, the churches, the schools, and the military-industrial complex. They challenge their elders to live by their values and creeds and at the same time to be sensitive to change and new occurrences. To act justly and to express genuine caring for others, one must consider the evolving demands of the environment, both the human and physical. Since there is no way to define this context in advance, there can be no assurance that prior principles will continue to apply. Certain basic values, however, are always relevant and applicable. It is the raising of our standards of performance in the light of the continuous reinterpretation of these values that constitutes human progress.

Values—the relative and the universal

To consider values from the standpoint of the relation between the actual and the ideal leads to another pair of aspects—the universal and the relative. These may be illustrated by a problem of great urgency, the need of all mankind to develop a sense of brotherhood and common destiny. The small world created by technology and by the overcrowding which has resulted in part from medical advances has meant that as human beings we became neighbors before we developed a world community. Can we become brothers in time to save ourselves? This is a question of life and death. Is there any way to resolve it? Everywhere around us the relative is immediately observable. Skins vary in color, food habits differ, marriage customs are numerous. But are there overriding commonalities? Does all mankind everywhere possess, or strive for, common values which can create a single community? Are universals discernible—whether at the foundations of our existence or at the highest levels of our soarings? If they are, can they unite that which is so discrepant and diverse?

These questions involve the large and fundamental issue: Are values always relative or do some apply universally? If the former, it is impossible to speak of any hierarchy as valid for others than those of us who adhere to it or outside of the specific culture in which we find ourselves. In that case, values are inescapably relativistic, particular and parochial. The alternative is that all humanity has a common standard for evaluating individual and social improvement.

This dichotomy, a source of perennial controversy among philosophers and social thinkers, is a good example of the propensity we all have to draw distinctions which hold up in the categories of logic, but do not hold true in the complexities of life. For the solution to the issue propounded above may be that the question has been wrongly stated. When such a dichotomy is presented—that is, when it is initially postulated that a value is either relative or universal—the character of the conclusions may be vitiated by the prior assumption. As in answering true-false questions on examinations, no other alternatives are allowable. Yet for all social questions there are no simple or final answers.

Again we must conclude that the nature of truth is not Either-Or but Both-And. In other words, values can be both relative and universal. Many thinkers, particularly the mystics, have always seen reality in this way. Recently this kind of thinking has found its way into the halls of science. Niels Bohr, the Danish physicist, who was familiar with the ideas of Soren Kierkegaard and William James, called it the complementarity principle. He proposed this to resolve the controversy among physicists concerning the nature of the electron. Is it a wave or a particle? Separate observations had revealed the electron behaving as one or the other; but it could not be observed to be both simultaneously. Hence it was assumed that the two interpretations were mutually exclusive. Bohr suggested, however, that wave and particle are "complementary opposites," so that the electron would be more completely described if both aspects were combined in a higher synthesis.[44]

In all modes of thought, efforts to simplify and systematize make it impossible to include the diversity that is characteristic of real life situations. Consequently, if the demands of logical consistency block our insight into reality, we should be ready to sacrifice the logic. Consistency, as Emerson said, can be "the hobgoblin of little minds. . . . With consistency a great soul has simply nothing to do."

These conceptions closely parallel those of field theory. This holds that no one part can be separated from the other parts of a field except by symbolic manipulation. In its ultimate sense, the field is without limits or boundaries, within or without, in space or time. At every moment, whether one wills this or not, the individual is changing the situation and conversely, the situation is changing the individual. As Bohr observed: "In the drama of existence we are ourselves both actors and spectators."

Humanistic and existential psychologists hold views similar to

*The reductionist is the person who solves the
dilemma [desire for coherence, while recognizing
the diversity that is truth] by favoring coherence over
adequacy. He is willing to blind himself, per-
manently or temporarily, to the complexities of his
subject in order to reap the rewards of rationalism.
The pluralist, on the other hand, is willing to
sacrifice rational coherence in order to keep alive his
recognition of diversity and subtlety. The eclectic
can use ideas from various systems of thought—can
put two opposing theories side by side.... Nothing
that seems true in any context can be denied,
not even if these special truths fail to cohere.*

*In the psychology of William James we encounter
many paradoxes of this order. His hospitable mind
was able in different contexts to give assent to
determinism and also freedom; to mentalism and to
physicalism; to parallelism and to interactionism. He
both affirmed and denied the unconscious; he
expressed both hope and despair concerning the
future of psychology as a science.*

Gordon W. Allport, "Imagination in Psychology: Some Needed
Steps," in Jacob Bronowski et al., *Imagination and the
University*, Toronto: University of Toronto Press, 1964.
(York University Invitation Lecture Series, 1963.)

---

those of the field theorists. They, too, envisage the individual as
interacting with his context—both influencing and being influenced
by it. This happens in many ways—by what we say, by how we say
it, and by what we are. Thus each mind influences that of others,
and new world views are created by such interacting thoughts. A
new metaphysic appeared when James Jeans departed from the
Newtonian view, that the world is a great machine, and characterized it as a great thought.[45] What each of us conceptualizes not only
becomes a self-realizing image for ourselves, but also creates prophecies and expectancies for others. Many physical and life scientists
no longer see nature as something entirely independent from them-

Spiritual progress is always in an ascending spiral.
. . . Ultimately, nothing is irrelevant to anything
else. There is a togetherness of all things in an endless
hierarchy of living and interacting patterns.

Aldous Huxley, *Adonis and the Alphabet and Other Essays,*
London: Chatto and Windus, 1956, p. 129.

---

selves; and among students of human society there are those who no
longer view individuals or groups of people as distinct and separate
entities. For the universalist, of course, everything—as Aldous
Huxley said—is related to everything else.

As these tendencies to more holistic, more fluid thinking increase,
as boundaries melt and the self and the not-self merge, some Western thinkers are beginning to point out the inadequacy of linear
thought and show more understanding of the mind-frame of the
Eastern mystics. Marshall McLuhan has noted how our thoughts
have been constricted by the two-dimensionality of the printed
word.[46] His contention has been that the "Global Village" of the
television screen offers a more complete view of what is going on
than do the printed pages of the newspaper. Directly and vividly we
see that Eastern and Western sentiments come together at many
crossroads. John Ciardi's observation that "It takes less time to see
a springtime than to write about one" is one variation of the ancient
theme expressed by Confucius: "A picture is worth a thousand
words."

Once new ways of thinking are legitimized, once it is accepted
that boundaries can vanish and multiple impressions can merge,
values can evolve and people can change. New kinds of relationships
come to be understood and prized. At least the understanding and
valuing seem new because the depth, details and dimensions are
different. But at the same time, such differences are viewed, in
Spinoza's phrase, under the guise of eternity. The most telling example of this is the permanent, yet continually changing, relationship
between the human species and the rest of our physical environment. Although there are elements of fluidity, the balance of nature
is an ultimate value. As Thomas B. Colwell has said: "The balance
of nature is . . . a *natural* norm, not a product of human convention
or supernatural authority."[47]

A student of Zen, in working with his master, Yusutani-Roshi, asked what was barring his way to enlightenment. Roshi replied:

"Consider these flowers in the bowl on this table. You look at them and exclaim: 'Oh, how beautiful these flowers are!' That is one kind of seeing. But when you see them, not as apart from you, but as yourself, you are enlightened."

Still failing to understand why he could not become enlightened, the student again asked what kept him from seeing things as he should. Came the response:

"Your enemy is your discursive thinking, it leads you to differentiate yourself on one side of an imaginary boundary from what is not you on the other side of this non-existent line."[48]

CHAPTER THREE

Foundations for a universal hierarchy of values

Biological, psychological, and anthropological bases

All human beings are different from one another, but all share the same fundamental needs. These needs result from both deficiencies and potentialities. The former occur because of an emptiness that wants to be filled. When it is filled, such a need is satisfied—at least for the time being. Our potentialities also call out for development; but, unlike needs, they are never satisfied. The more we use them, the greater is the delight we take in their continuing use. It is the lure that scaling heights has for the mountain climber. But in human growth, though we reach peak after peak, there is never a final summit. The upper limits are forever unknown, unseen.

Our organism welcomes whatever can meet a deficiency or fulfill a potentiality, and calls it good. Regardless of the nature of the need—be it potentiality or deficiency—there are many ways of meeting it. Since we may select from among these, a range of choice is always open to us. Such choices entail preferences and priorities, and it is to these that we attach value.

Certain physical needs must obviously be satisfied if life is to be maintained. These are deficiencies which want to be filled. Food,

*If B-values are as necessary as vitamins and love,
and if their absence can make you sick, then what
people have talked about for thousands of years as
the religious or platonic or rational life seems to
be a very basic part of human nature. Man is a
hierarchy of needs, with the biological needs at the
base of the hierarchy and the spiritual needs at
the top. Unlike the biological needs, however, the
B-values are not hierarchical in and of themselves.
One is as important as the next, and each one can be
defined in terms of all the others. Truth, for
example, must be complete, aesthetic, comprehensive,
and strangely enough, it must be funny in an
Olympian god-like sense. Beauty must be true, good,
comprehensive, etc.*

Abraham H. Maslow, *Goals of Humanistic Education*,
typescript of presentation at Esalen, September 1968, p. 9.

---

clothing, sleep, sex and shelter are examples which each culture
satisfies differently. The Australian Blackfellow wears no clothing
even during the chill nights in the Out-Back of central Australia, but
seeks the comfort of the warm ground and the glowing coals of a
waning fire. In contrast, the Eskimo has walled himself off from
vastly more severe climatic conditions by the world's most ingenious
thermal clothing and his virtually heat-tight igloos. Both native
groups survive remarkably well, and both, in strikingly different
ways, seek the same objective—protection from the rigors of the
cold.

More remarkable perhaps are the outer limits of physical potentialities. These appear, according to the scientist René Dubos,[49] to be
the common genetic heritage of mankind and yet to be only slightly
developed among most members of the species. In response to needs,
our potentialities often emerge to an extraordinary degree. Through
his acutely tuned senses the Blackfellow, living in a semi-desert, can
fathom out hidden water holes and even judge the amount of water
accurately before it is seen. Similarly, a blind person can measure
distances and depths by the "feel" of the air. Vision, too, can be

His senses were acute . . . and there was a wonderful
fitness of body and mind. He could pace sixteen
rods more accurately than another man could measure
them with rod and chain. He could find his path in
the woods at night, he said, better by his feet
than his eyes. He could estimate the measure of a
tree very well by the eye . . . he could estimate
the weight of a calf or a pig, like a dealer. From a box
containing a bushel or more of loose pencils, he
could take up with his hands fast enough just a dozen
pencils at every grasp. . . . He knew the country
like a fox or a bird, and passed through it as freely
by paths of his own. He knew every track in the
snow or on the ground, and what creature had taken
this path before him. . . . His power of observation
seemed to indicate additional senses. He saw as
with microscope, heard as with ear-trumpet, and his
memory was a photographic register of all he saw
and heard. Every fact lay in glory in his mind, a type
of the order and beauty of the whole.

Ralph Waldo Emerson, "Thoreau," *Complete Essays,*
op. cit., pp. 900–06.

---

trained to extend far beyond its usual range. An example is the naturalist who can detect minute changes in the physical environment.

Potentiality responds to need when individuals summon unusual strength in times of crisis. Relatively small women have lifted cars or other heavy objects to release a pinned-down victim. Obviously such physical possibilities do not have to remain inaccessible and unused. Nor do they have to be reserved only for those rare situations which make such great demands upon the organism that they break through the walls erected around most potentialities by habit or disuse. The same may be said of the border areas in which the physical and psychological both reside. William James, for instance, writing on the "second wind,"[50] suggests that most of us have great funds of endurance and energy available after initial fatigue is felt.

The point is that the person must value the "second wind" if he is to utilize it sufficiently, and then through virtuosity go the extra mile.

When we explore the realm of the psychological, it is apparent that there are needs and possibilities just as fundamental as the physical. These, too, are common to all mankind, and form a hierarchy from lower to higher, from deficiencies to potentialities. Maslow has demonstrated that we function at our very best, are healthiest, and are developing our capacities to the fullest when we are actualizing the values which stand highest in intellectual, aesthetic, and spiritual terms—namely, love, goodness, truth, beauty, and justice. But, as in the area of the physical, we are apt to disregard the range of our potential in these spheres because we are not properly self-aware. The result is that we do not use our psychological capacity because we do not know it is there. Paul Goodman might be thought extreme in claiming that people characteristically use only 2 percent of their abilities; and James Coleman, similarly, could be overstating the case when he asserts that most high school students are learning for only ten minutes out of the school day.[51] Nevertheless, such estimates are too common, and contain too much truth, to be ignored.

The incontestable fact remains that all of us have great capacities which we could call upon at will if we so desired. The question then is: Why do we not choose these options? Is it that we do not even know that we could make these choices? If all of us possess great unused potentialities, what are the even greater forces that dam up the springs of attribute and will? What keeps them from flowing at freshet strength?

Both Abraham Maslow and Sidney Jourard suggest that a barrier is erected by the fact that, in becoming socialized, we also become alienated from ourselves. Normality numbs us. We lose our ability to directly experience ourselves psychologically and biologically. In addition, we lose contact with others and with nature. Neither physically nor psychologically do we reach in or out. We forget, as Herbert Read has reminded us:

> "What is common to the psychic structure of mankind is the only secure foundation for a community of behaviour and aspiration."[52]

Our contacts with other human beings can affect us in different ways. Society may serve as a prison, cramping and confining each unique personality to a common, predetermined shape. This was

*During the first few weeks of life, a baby is not
"human" in the sense we are here using that word.
The infant is equipped with enough reflexes to
keep him alive, but he is little more than an alimentary
canal with arms and legs attached. . . . At a few
weeks of age, a baby begins to respond to the human
beings in his environment. He does not know that
they are "father" or "mother." He does not know any
words, any symbols. The process may be regarded
as central to universal human nature precisely
because it is beyond language, which is to say beyond
culture. The first building block of humanness is
responsiveness to the human presence. . . . The parent
is delighted by the baby's signs of nascent humanness. She shows her delight. She smiles, laughs, sings,
talks to the baby. He responds to her response. He
begins to reply to her smiles with smiles of his
own. His squeals, gurgles, cooing and crowing begin
to grow purposeful rather than random. They
convey an unmistakeable feeling-state. The parent
responds with a heightened and corresponding
feeling-state, which she communicates through expressions, gestures, inflections of voice, squeals, gurgles,
cooing and crowing of her own. And so the process
builds, and spirals, and soars.*

*This universal form of communication is of the
very essence of becoming and remaining a human
being. It is the bedrock on which the rest of the
human structure is erected.*

Henry Anderson, "The Nature of Human Nature," Part I:
"Sympathetic Interaction," *Manas*, April 1, 1970, pp. 1–2.

---

what Rousseau thought, and Wordsworth also had this in mind
when he wrote: "Shades of the prison-house begin to close upon
the growing boy."[53] But we should remember that it is only through
society that we are liberated and civilized. The humanization of an

infant, as Henry Anderson has argued, begins in the family with its first, early, intimate contacts with parents. Later, to enrich our minds and deepen our sensibilities, we need access to books, painting, music, and the other arts which are preserved and passed on through social institutions.

If we treasure health (not just the absence of illness), and the joy of intellectual discovery (not just getting our work done), we should, as Jourard says, "redefine values by which men live, to satisfy more needs and to acknowledge more self than is presently the case."[54] Our failure to do so is due, at least in part, to our theorists, educators, and researchers. But the media and the arts fall equally short in providing food for the soul. Their messages, as Joseph Wood Krutch remarked, are all too often "counsels of despair."[55] Bertrand Russell claimed that we "imagined ourselves into littleness, darkness, ignorance." It was his counsel that we should "imagine ourselves back into light."[56] Too often, our social prophets speak of doom and apocalypse; too rarely, of promise and potentialities. As we have seen, the Freudians have generally ignored the human capacity for goodness and transcendence. Nor can the experimental psychologists accept these higher values within their chosen frame of reference. Characteristically, their focus is the reductionistic study of human beings in piecemeal ways and only in terms of objective evidence. What is not seen does not exist; what cannot be measured does not count.

Not all social scientists, however, arrive at such depressing images of mankind. Many do not believe, with the relativists, that every ethical system simply reflects the values of a particular culture and has no wider reference. Morris Ginsberg contends that relativists exaggerate the variations and underestimate the resemblances. His studies of comparative sociology disclosed much that is similar in the basic morality of the primitive and the civilized. The list of moral elements which are common to all known societies includes the prohibition of homicide within a well-defined sphere; rules forbidding violence or bodily injury to the person, as well as attacks on honor and reputation; and the condemnation of pride and arrogance. Everywhere, Ginsberg found, positive approval is given to doing good and furthering the well-being of others, to mutual aid and generosity, to telling the truth and keeping promises, and to property rights in some form or other.

Diversities in moral judgments are explicable, in his view, by the differences in the moral importance of the "same" acts in different social situations or institutional frameworks. The same act might thus be considered moral in one situation and either non-moral or immoral in another. Polygamy or polyandry, for instance, may be justified by societies where one sex is in oversupply.[57]

Further testimony from a wide variety of sources supports the view that all of us share in certain universal traits and that we acknowledge or aspire to the same higher values. Clyde Kluckhohn concluded that certain values unite mankind across cultural boundaries and inferred that these form "some basis for human agreement on what is desirable for the furtherance of life." He pointed out that there is in all societies an interdiction against "killing, indiscriminate lying and stealing within the in-group," and in fact, against whatever might bring about disruption or destruction within the social unit.[58] The same basic conclusion is reached by those who have conducted comparative studies of the young. Thus Lawrence Kohlberg's research on "The Child as a Moral Philosopher" revealed much similarity in the stages of character development of children in several cultures.[59] Correspondingly, Norman Kiell demonstrated from his cross-cultural study of adolescents in different historical periods that, while their experience does vary "in its more specific aspects," yet there is a "common factor in its more general characteristics." In his judgment, "the basic affective and biosocial life of the adolescent is universal for virtually all cultures and throughout time."[60] All this research indicates a convergence on a universal ideal of the Good Person.

It is not surprising, therefore, that the same result emerges from studies of opinions about teachers. In his work with illiterates, Frank Laubach found that learners tend to coincide in their statements about what makes a good teacher—their ideal type being the one who treats each student "like a Rajah." A Harris poll based on a large sample of American high school students in 1969 disclosed remarkable unanimity in their characterization of the "good teacher."[61] In this light we can understand the international odyssey which Danny Kaye undertook some years ago on behalf of UNICEF. Visiting school after school in many countries where he could not speak the language, this gifted man everywhere achieved immediate empathy with children. The universal appeal of his compassionate humor easily transcended the barriers of speech.

The new humanists, in contrast, have tended to give the whole individual a central role and in this way to include the inner person as well as the outer. Will, purpose, and decision-making thus become important. Human beings are credited with an imagination—one of the qualities which not only differentiate us from other species, but also link each person with all others. Contemporary thinkers are paying renewed attention to the variety of bonds we have with our fellowmen.

The structural anthropologist Claude Lévi-Strauss has shown how people are united throughout the world. Language—under which he includes speech, music, art, ritual, myth, religion, literature, cooking, trading—reflects a universal human need to communicate and a universal desire to attach meaning to things, to find order and thus to organize the chaos of the universe. He speculates that there is a least common denominator of human thought, and that the origin of human speech and of human society may have occurred at one time. Perhaps this was the critical period when humanity emerged, and, with it, as the anthropologist Alfred L. Kroeber believed, the "psychic unity of mankind." In similar vein, Noam Chomsky refers to a universal syntax which is inherited by each human being. Studying languages as a mirror of consciousness, he contends that, although they differ in their surface structure, translation from one to another would be impossible if they did not share a deep common structure, the equivalent of a "universal grammar." This would seem to be what Abraham Lincoln intuitively perceived when he alluded to "the mystic chords of memory," and what L. T. Hobhouse meant by the "Central Mind." C. G. Jung, discussing the "collective unconscious" and universal archetypes, has concluded that individuals who are free and healthy can draw upon a "psychic non-ego" which unites each of us with other humans and with nature.

These concepts and hypotheses lead us to a significantly expanded image of humanity. By reaching out to all mankind and to the non-human world as well, we can transcend ourselves; and, as we do this, we exhibit qualities that are inimitably human. Through possessing an imagination, we live not only in the present, but in the past and the future. We conjure up utopias and dream of golden ages. Barriers of time and space are no longer insurmountable. The walls are taken away. Such thoughts, as Emerson knew, "find us always young and keep us so."

The ethical basis

One perennial source of values and of their arrangement in a hierarchy can be found in religious teaching and moral philosophy. All

*In essentials the moral systems of the world show
striking similarities. A list of virtues or duties drawn
up by a Buddhist would not differ very greatly
from one drawn up by a Christian, a Confucianist,
a Muhammadan, or a Jew. Formally all the ethico-
religious systems are universalist in scope. . . .
But the formal resemblance is deceptive. The univer-
salism is never thoroughgoing and is variously
limited.*

*The higher religions converge in their teaching
on the inward nature of morality and the universality
of love and its obligations. The philosophers, after
the manner of their trade, emphasize their differences
from each other. But in their accounts of the good
for man they move within a restricted circle of ideas
—happiness, wisdom, virtue, fulfillment.*

Morris Ginsberg, "On the Diversity of Morals," from *Essays
in Sociology and Social Philosophy*, Harmondsworth, England:
Penguin Books, 1968, pp. 245, 264–65.

the principal religions of mankind, like all ethical systems, incorpo-
rate an image of humanity as we could be if we were to develop our
potentialities to the highest. These ideals are statements not of what
is, but of what ought to be. They are extrapolations beyond present
reality to an ultimate ideal of perfection ("Be ye perfect, even as
your Father in heaven is perfect"). As such, values are goals for
human endeavor and models to guide our growth. "It is of the
essence of ideals," says Ralph Barton Perry, "that they should be
unattainable. They define not what men possess but what they
seek."[62]

Like the social scientists who discern similarities among diversities,
moral philosophers and religious leaders are far from being unani-
mous in the ethical doctrines they teach or preach. But on certain
basic points, their views converge toward a consensus. In general,
they envisage human beings as compounded of the biological and
the spiritual, as an animal species somehow kindled by a spark from
a more than mortal fire. They therefore urge us to allow what is

good within us to emerge, and to live in peace and amity with our fellowmen.

That there is this degree of consensus is manifestly important, and it is something that cultural relativists do not and simply cannot explain. The similarities in the conception of the higher virtues held by Buddhists, Christians, Confucians, Jews and Muslims cannot be understood except in terms which are basic to human nature and thus universal to all. Doubtless it was this truth—a truth extending beyond the rational to the realm of the mystical—which has inspired a number of poets and philosophers to affirm their belief in a common bond which links men together, thereby coming intuitively to the same conclusion as an increasing number of scientists.

This belief has been expressed in various ways—many of them non-verbal. Rousseau, for instance, postulated in his concept of the General Will that one and the same interest unites all members of a group (a notion whose logic can be extended to include the entire human race) and that all people would consciously will this if they were sufficiently enlightened in their judgment. The General Will is always good; its mistakes are due to its being uninformed and unenlightened. Rousseau held the Socratic belief that right conduct depends on knowledge, and that when you know the good you do not choose the bad. Following him, Blake conceived of all mankind united in the Infinite. "Everything that lives" he proclaimed, "is holy." His was the vision that was able

> To see a world in a Grain of Sand
> And a Heaven in a Wild Flower
> Hold Infinity in the palm of your hand
> And Eternity in an hour.

Emerson, too, spoke of "that Unity, that Over-Soul, within which every man's particular being is contained and made one with every other."

In this case, as with other values, practice is a long way from precept. Although we may discern the infinite in each particular, it is true that the habits, and at times the social conventions, of a specific culture appear to contradict the universal ethic. There is a saying which makes explicit what many imply by their actions: "I love mankind. It's just people that I can't stand."

Those who study mankind in the microcosm cannot but observe the deviations from the ideal of universal brotherhood which religious and philosophical leaders prescribe for the macrocosm. A country may publicly profess an ethic which embraces the Commandment "Thou shalt not kill." But private citizens by the millions keep guns in their homes or on their persons, and apparently are ready to use them. Moreover, their government engages in war, conscripts its youth for military service, and orders them to kill other human beings whom it calls "the enemy." Jules Henry, in a work with the significant title *Culture Against Man*, discusses the effects of the "socialization process" in the schools.[63] In his view, the schools emphasize winning more than working together and sharing. "A competitive culture," he states, "endures by tearing people down." In such a situation the slower children come to envy, or even hate, the brighter ones and are induced to cheat as their only way to get the good grades demanded by their parents or their own pride. Maslow is similarly critical of the conventional morality which merely conforms in externals to accepted values. Should such conduct be designated as moral or as which he has termed the "pervasive psychopathology of the average"? "The ordinary ethical behavior of the average person," he maintains, "is largely conventional behavior rather than truly ethical."[64]

Conduct that is truly ethical has to adhere consciously to a higher principle rather than merely adjust to an external code. The danger in the latter is that people will depart from a code whenever they think that this is to their advantage and can be done with impunity. A case in point is our willingness to speak the truth. Admittedly this is one of the higher values, but we well know that it is regularly and deliberately violated. This is confirmed by the research which one of us has conducted into the attitudes and beliefs of gifted high school students. At least one group of adolescents discounted the value of truth. Many of those who described themselves as social leaders said they were willing to lie and cheat, if these actions were in their self-interest. In contrast, most students who called themselves creative intellectuals or studious thought such behavior was wrong in any context.[65]

Some of those who have studied the process of socialization have concluded that much that society does inhibits or destroys the natural goodness inherent in the child. The Scottish psychiatrist, R. D. Laing, insists this is the case:

> "By the time a new human being is 15 or so . . . we are left with a being just like ourselves, a half-crazed creature more or less adjusted to a mad world. This is normality."[66]

In general, however, researchers and writers in the social sciences and education operate from the premise that the adult knows best and that the child must be trained to be loving and good, honest and true, that is, ethical in the sense in which the adult interprets these terms. As John Rich puts it, "Most rules are developed by adults and then transmitted to children." Many who study the growth of character feel this is as it should be. Although he accepts Maslow's concept of self-actualization as representing an ideal direction of growth, Rich also talks about moral growth and social orientation as being related to winning and following more clearly defined roles. "Between the ages of seven and eight," he reports, "a less egocentric and more socially oriented outlook develops. The child now tries to win, . . ."[67] although it is not clear why trying to win should be called "less egocentric" and "more socially oriented."

These contradictions between professed values and actual practice have their effect on such a concept as brotherhood. At a universal level, this would appear to mean that all persons on the face of the earth are created equal and have certain inalienable rights. On the ways in which mankind has applied equality, however, the comment has been made: "Yes, but some are more equal than others." Thus the Pilgrims, whose lives were presumably motivated by a desire to be both good and God-fearing, have been criticized by other Americans for their lack of ethics in dealing with the American Indians. Mark Twain's trenchant statement summarizes that thinking: "First the Pilgrims fell on their knees and then they fell on the aborigines."

How we erect an ethical hierarchy can be examined further. Most of the researchers and theorists who develop hierarchies apparently believe that civilized adults are more moral than children, primitive people and—of course—animals. Yet there are others who would upend the ladder or place it on the ground. A. S. Neill, the creator of the free school, Summerhill, has claimed that children are loving, not cruel, when they are in their natural state and adults do not interfere. Self-regulation results in less aggression than does a morality imposed by adult rules. A follow-up study of Summerhill graduates seems to support his view.[68] Ashley Montagu also challenges the idea that mankind is necessarily selfish and competitive, arguing instead that we are by nature cooperative.[69]

Is there evidence that primitive people, those who by Western criteria are uncivilized, can live together peacefully and civilly? A Micronesian chieftain has been quoted as saying:

"Before the foreigner came we lived in peace. The forest fed us—simply but sufficiently. We did not work. Is work a virtue when nothing is to be gained by it? Neighbours were friendly.

Children obedient. Life was a tradewind without gusts or squalls. But now comes struggle—struggle for money. Money for what? We do not need clothing—the sunshine clothes us. We do not need an iron roof to carry water into a cement tank. The water that streams down the trunk of a tree can be turned into a jar."[70]

In a natural society, as Read says, there is no distinction between the psychology of work and play. But in many technologically advanced countries obeying the Puritan tradition, to work is good and "the devil finds work for idle hands to do." Among primitive people, as various anthropologists have noted, a way is ordinarily found to feed all in the tribe, by communal sharing of the available food. Yet in recent years, it has become increasingly apparent to thoughtful people in the civilized world that many human beings are allowed to go hungry. On the world level, perhaps more than half of mankind is hungry, while vast numbers are actually starving. Even in such a wealthy nation as the United States it is estimated that at least a fifth have insufficient food and many are seriously malnourished. Anthropologists have even gone so far as to question the ability of civilized man or woman to love. Robert Lowie claims that there is "almost a direct ratio between rudeness of culture and gentleness with children."[71] Read attributes what he calls "the superior cohesion of primitive societies" to the fact that they "evolve their patterns from the collective unconscious."

How shall we fathom the basic qualities of human nature? When we observe our contemporary civilization, how can we disentangle our fundamental human-ness from the complex network of institutions, values, and behavior patterns—the culture or society—in which modern mankind is enveloped?

One way, as we have just seen, is to study children before they are too much altered (whether for good or bad) by the processes of socialization. Another method is to compare sophisticated humanity —the civilized ones, as we designate ourselves—with our primitive contemporaries who are assuredly closer to nature and therefore might be assumed to exhibit what is essential to human nature. A third way is to look outside the human species to the other animals, particularly to our closest relatives, the apes, and to see what they are like. Ever since the dawn of literature, poetically-minded people have been attributing specific human traits to certain animals—the cunning fox, the courageous lion, the savage tiger, the wise owl, the gentle fawn, the faithful dog, and so on. But there is also the reverse image of ascribing to humanity traits which are thought to be characteristic of other animals. How these traits are conceived varies according to each writer's selection, emphasis, and subsequent generalization.

Charles Darwin's findings and larger hypotheses gave currency to the fact that the human species is a product of a long evolution, and explained it all as the result of the survival of the fittest in a struggle for existence. Social Darwinites applied this notion to human society, developing such ideas as one finds in Herbert Spencer—a Hobbesian painting in nineteenth-century dress. More recently, a school of writers (whom we could call "zoological determinists") have been busy interpreting the present stage of human evolution in conformity with assumptions about our early beginnings. The common theme is this: we are basically animals, and bad animals in the bargain, as were our ancestors. Hostility, aggression, killing, are deeply rooted in our nature. We are such, and thus we behave, from biological compulsion.

Examples which may be cited are Konrad Lorenz's *On Aggression* and Desmond Morris's *The Naked Ape*, both of which portray our species as aggressive animals. Indeed, they give short shrift to those of our qualities which are distinctively human—the ability to dream and plan ahead, our symbolic talents, the faculty of imagination, our religion and art, and so on. Similarly, Robert Ardrey in *African Genesis* develops the theory that *Homo sapiens* evolved from carnivorous, predatory killer apes and that our age-old affinity for war and weapons is the natural result of this inherited animal instinct. He rejects the view that the human being has an innate talent for living creatively and peacefully, but has gradually degenerated as the race became "civilized." To speak of mankind as being born good, but being destroyed by the adult society and its institutions is dangerous talk. Instead Ardrey believes that we should congratulate ourselves on the progress we have made as we have emerged from our unlikely origins. In his words:

> "Man is a predator whose natural instinct is to kill with a weapon. . . . We were born of risen apes, not fallen angels, and the apes were armed killers besides. . . . The miracle of man is not how far he has sunk but how magnificently he has risen. We are known among the stars by our poems, not our corpses."[72]

The Social Darwinists and the zoological determinists, however, do not go unchallenged. Both the facts they select and the inferences they draw are questioned by those who contend that such theories

*Pervading all nature we may see at work a stern
discipline, which is a little cruel that it may be very
kind. That state of universal warfare maintained
throughout the lower creation, to the great perplexity
of many worthy people, is at bottom the most
merciful provision which the circumstances admit of.
It is much better that the ruminant animal, when
deprived by age of the vigor which made its existence
a pleasure, should be killed by some beast of prey,
than that it should linger out a life made painful by
infirmities, and eventually die of starvation. . . .
Meanwhile the well-being of existing humanity, and
the unfolding of it into this ultimate perfection,
are both secured by that same beneficent, though
severe discipline, to which the animate creation
at large is subject: a discipline which is pitiless in the
working out of good; a felicity-pursuing law which
never swerves for the avoidance of partial and
temporary suffering. The poverty of the incapable,
the distresses that come upon the imprudent, the
starvation of the idle, and those shoulderings aside of
the weak by the strong, which leave so many "in
shallows and in miseries," are the decrees of a large,
far-seeing benevolence. . . . Nevertheless, when
regarded not separately, but in connection with the
interests of universal humanity, these harsh fatalities
are seen to be full of the highest beneficence . . .
the same beneficence which brings to early graves the
children of diseased parents, and singles out the
low-spirited, the intemperate, and the debilitated as
the victims of an epidemic.*

Herbert Spencer, *Social Statics*, London: Chapman and Hall,
1850, Part III, Chap. 25, p. 322.

---

*"Don't compete!—competition is always injurious
to the species, and you have plenty of reasons to avoid
it!" That is the tendency of nature, not always
realized in full, but always present. That is the
watchword which comes to us from the bush, the
forest, the river, the ocean. Therefore combine
—practice mutual aid! That is the surest means for
giving to each and all the greatest safety, the best
guarantee of existence and progress, bodily,
intellectual and moral. That is what nature teaches
us; and that is what all those animals which have
attained the highest position in their respective
classes have done. That is also what man—the most
primitive man—has been doing; and that is why
man has reached the position upon which we stand
now. . . .*

Peter Kropotkin, *Mutual Aid, A Factor of Evolution,*
New York: Alfred A. Knopf, 1925, from the end of chapter 2.

---

misunderstand the true nature of humanity and of other animals
besides. Some of those who have studied the lives of animals have
noted the high degree of cooperation found within a given species. In
fact, animals rarely kill wantonly or in mass as do human beings.
Peter Kropotkin, for example, made extensive studies of animal behavior in the late 19th century. As a young man, this Russian prince
became disillusioned with government-imposed discipline and had
second thoughts about other issues while serving five years in Siberia
with a Cossack cavalry regiment. It was during this time, when
Darwin's *Origin of Species* was the talk of intellectual Europe, that
he observed the habits of wild animals. From his first-hand observations, Kropotkin concluded that the savage laws of social Darwinism
did not apply to the creatures which he had seen in their natural
habitat as gentle and loving. He noted that mutual aid was practiced
among higher animals, even among the carnivorous ones. Insufficient
attention had been given, in his view, to the cooperation that exists
on all rungs of the ladder of evolution, and increases among the more

advanced species. Hence, he inferred that mankind could learn from them some lessons in wise behavior.

Various of the more recent investigations into the behavior of animals have also given an ethically favorable verdict. W. C. Allee has argued that we humans might profit by modeling our own behavior on that of animals:

"An organization of the nations of the world devoted primarily to meeting these and similar human needs would be based on the great drive toward natural altruism that extends throughout the whole animal kingdom."[73]

That "war is not in our genes" is the thesis of Sally Carrighar who has spent more than thirty years observing animals in their native habitats. Rather, she concludes, our propensity to war and to aggression in general is what we learn after we are born and is fostered by our social institutions. Animals, in fact, are much less prone to kill other members of their own species than is commonly supposed. The belief to the contrary rests on exaggerated generalization or on the study of animals in captivity where the strain of confinement and over-crowding induces unnatural hostility. There is, then, no biological imperative which necessitates that human beings should be "killer apes." We do, however, have a cultural inheritance, linked to "the irritations of being crowded" which manifests itself in hostility toward others of our own kind. The fault lies in our bad institutions and the habits they generate.[74]

The aesthetic basis

If we possess qualities which make our species distinctively human and so differentiate us from the other animals, evidence for this should appear in the products of the imagination. For we are never more human than when we dream our dreams. The ethical characteristics which mankind shares—the valuing of justice and goodness—are paralleled by the taste for beauty.

Psychological studies have shown that people react negatively to, and are depressed in, ugly surroundings. A beautiful environment, on the other hand, is uplifting and inspiring. There are universal reports about the peak experiences that occur in sublime settings, when one seems to stand outside oneself, as the word ecstasy literally means. Though there are variations in style and taste from

---

century to century, and from civilization to civilization, the love of
beauty itself is endemic, ubiquitous, inextinguishable.

All literate peoples have celebrated beauty in poetry and song,
particularly the beauty of nature. Likewise, in the oral ballad tradition, there is much evidence that both the preliterate and illiterate
have always been moved by the mystery and wonder of it all. Prehistoric burial mounds have been found to contain the remains of
dried plants that best answer to the descriptions of flowers. This is
a theme which Lydia Maria Child, the abolitionist poet, has univer-
salized, pointing out that all peoples have blessed flowers, wreathing
them "round the cradle, the marriage-altar and the tomb." A delight
in flowers, she observed, unites the Indian child of the Far West and
the Persian of the East.[75]

In the drama *Prometheus Bound*, when the hero is tortured for
bringing to mankind the fire he had stolen from heaven, Aeschylus
has him invoke the elemental forces of nature—earth, sun, sea and
sky—with which he feels kinship.

> Oh sky divine where winds fly swift of wing;
> Ye fountain springs of rivers; and ocean waves
> Whose smiles pass counting; earth, mother of all;

To you, and the sun's all-seeing orb, I speak—
Behold what I, a god, from gods do suffer.[76]

The Roman poet Lucretius, writing *On the Nature of Things,* opens his work with an invocation to Venus, the symbol of life, creation and beauty both in the physical world and among humans. The Duke, in Shakespeare's *As You Like It,* sounds much like one of today's hippies as he praises the life of simplicity and frugality. By dropping out of the power-oriented social system and rejecting conspicuous consumerism, one could return to the beauty of nature and thence to peace of mind. Not only would life take on new meaning (and perhaps a truer meaning), but the individual would also be more secure. As the Duke phrased it: "Are not these woods more free from peril than the envious court?"[77] For him, the Forest of Arden afforded the same kind of haven that Prospero found in the enchanted island of the *Tempest.* Nor should one forget that the myth of the divine creation, as it was imaginatively sketched in the Book of Genesis, placed Adam and Eve, while in their state of innocence, in a garden. The human species, in other words, is conceived as being harmoniously adapted to a naturally beautiful environment.

This is a topic to which art and thought continually return in the late 18th and 19th centuries. The conflict in values between material means (money, status, power) and spiritual ends (beauty, tranquillity, authenticity) was stressed repeatedly by the Romantic writers. Wordsworth stated this simply and directly in his poem, "The World":

The World is too much with us; late and soon,
Getting and spending, we lay waste our powers;
Little we see in Nature that is ours;
We have given our hearts away, a sordid boon!

He went on to say that we are unresponsive to nature's grandeur and that disharmony pervades our entire lives. "For this, for everything, we are out of tune." Such a feeling is akin to Emerson's thought that "The misery of man appears like childish petulance, when we explore the steady and prodigal provision that has been made for his support and delight on this green ball which floats him through the heavens."[78]

William Cullen Bryant saw the problem similarly and suggested that nature contained revitalizing forces:

Stranger, if thou has learned a truth needs
No school of long experience, that the world

Is full of guilt and misery, and has seen
Enough of all its sorrows, crimes, and cares,
To tire thee of it, enter this wild wood
And view the haunts of Nature . . .[79]

The naturalist John Muir believed that in nature one arrives at the center of meaning: "I'll interpret the rocks, learn the language of flood, storm and avalanche—and get as near the heart of the world as I can."[80] Tennyson, too, had this in mind when he reflected on the "flower in the crannied wall":

Little flower—but if I could understand
What you are, root and all, and all in all,
I should know what God and Man is.

For not only is the natural wonder of things revealed in the immensity of the sky, the broad expanse of earth, or the vastness of the ocean, but it is equally contained in the smallest of nature's handiworks—in "a leaf of grass" (Whitman) or "a grain of sand" (Blake).

So interpreted, our relationship with nature remains ever intimate and inseparable. Not only the air we breathe, but all of nature, is a vital part of mankind. Thus, unless we maintain communion with the nature which is our common birthright, we cannot become fully human or lead lives that are healthy and enriched. "To watch the corn grow, and the blossoms set" wrote Ruskin, "to draw hard breath over plowshare or spade; to read, to think, to love, to hope, to pray—these are the things that make men happy." For it is nature that enlivens the senses, gives pungency to perception, and immediacy to experience. "Climb the mountains," said Muir, "and get their good tidings. Nature's peace will flow into you as sunshine flows into trees."[81]

This mood of peace and joy, which a sense of harmony with nature universally evokes, has ever been a source of inspiration to the creative arts. In the Western world, that outpouring of genius in the late 18th and the 19th centuries which we call the Romantic movement owes much to such influences. Alike in literature, painting and music, this movement was committed to two great themes: that, because nature and humanity are good, we live best in harmony with nature, and that it is wholesome for us freely to express spontaneous feeling. The Romantics glorified the universal qualities which all persons have in common, even—or perhaps particularly—the most primitive and least lettered. These are the tendrils by which we touch one another and the roots that tie us to nature. It is these

The tradesman, the attorney comes out of the
din and craft of the street and sees the sky and the
woods, and is a man again. In their eternal calm,
he finds himself. The health of the eye seems
to demand a horizon. We are never tired, so long as
we can see far enough. . . . Every rational creature
has all nature for his dowry and estate. It is his, if he
will. He may divest himself of it, he may creep
into a corner, and abdicate his kingdom, as most men
do, but he is entitled to the world by his con-
stitution. . . . A work of art is an abstract or epitome
of the world. It is the result or expression of nature, in
miniature.

Ralph Waldo Emerson, "Essay on Nature" in *Complete Essays,*
op. cit., pp. 10–13.

---

which express for the Romantic the unity, the rhythm and the right-ness of it all.

In such beliefs, the complementarity of the subject and object, the actual and ideal, and the relative and universal, are clearly evident. For the aesthetic values of nature and of art are universal in appeal; but their myriad forms or styles are intimately tied to culture, time and place.

It was Rousseau, more than any other single person, who gave romanticism its launching impetus. Both primitive peoples and chil-dren, as he understood them, are easily—should one say "naturally"? —in tune with the natural. Only the "civilized," who have been cor-rupted by society and twisted by its institutions, have to make an effort to recapture the primal essence of the world in all its original goodness and beauty. The Romantic gospel spread quickly through-out the arts, across Europe and to the emerging United States, where the grandeur of the landscape and the omnipresence of the frontier made people receptive to the message. Thomas Jefferson—philoso-pher, scientist, architect, statesmen, and one of the geniuses of his age—expressed an unequivocal preference in his hierarchy of values:

"Those who labor in the earth are the chosen people of God if ever he had a chosen people, whose breasts He has made his peculiar deposit for substantial and genuine virtue. It is the focus in which he keeps alive that sacred fire, which otherwise might escape from the face of the earth. Corruption of morals in the mass of cultivators is a phenomenon of which no age nor nation has furnished an example."[82]

The love of the soil and of the occupation closest to it suggests that a life in harmony with nature and conforming to its ways is pure and wholesome. Thus the Romantics not only drew inspiration from the physical aspects of nature, but also extolled (idealized, perhaps) the folk-culture of the peasant. Painters filled their canvases with landscapes, poets communed with the elements, and composers wove into their symphonies the melodies of the folk-dance. What is more, the Romantic spirit appreciated those of mankind's works which bore the signs of use and had the touch of the antique. For what was more natural than to feel in the present a kinship with our own past?

Reverence for such values can be illustrated from many of the civilizations of mankind, notably those of Asia. When the doors of Japan were opened to the West, the country's ethos was thus described by the first American envoy. "There is an equal absence," wrote Townsend Harris in his diary, "of any appearance of wealth or of poverty—a state of things that may perhaps constitute the real happiness of the people. . . . It is more like the golden age of simplicity and honesty than I have seen in any other country."[83]

To this end, many of the traditional elements of Japanese culture contributed. Through the practice of Zen and its rituals, especially the tea ceremony, an effort was made to relate the life of the individual to the universe. The austerity and simplicity of these practices were felt to give humanity a release from the material concerns of life, which were held to obscure both ultimate and immediate reality. What was wanted was the barest life possible, the life of poverty, *wabi*. This was the direct route to basic truth and inherent beauty; and, seen from this viewpoint, the most ordinary materials —bare wood and rough clay—become works of art. A companion concept, *sabi*, refers to the beauty of age, and usually to a tranquil, lovely spot which has aged naturally. This term, as Heinrich Engel points out, is "frequently used in Buddhist scripts to designate ultimate liberation from worldly passions and sorrows . . . *nirvana*."[84] Through such approaches in their gardens, paintings and other art forms, Japanese artists try to present "the indescribable essence of the universe."

The universal quest for beauty and harmony is inspired by the earth on which we live, yet it is also transcendental. The latter aspect of romanticism is epitomized in the poetry and pictorial art of Blake, a man who was on easy and apparently direct terms with the mystical and the supernatural. Blake moved dramatically away from the classical and the Aristotelian, reinstating the Platonic and setting the stage for the American transcendentalists. Throughout his work, the infinite could be seen to permeate the smallest manifestations. "To hold Infinity in the palm of your hand" refers both to the One Infinite and to the myriad hands of all mankind outstretched throughout the world in supplication or celebration.

From this philosophy it is but a few steps to Shelly and Keats, Emerson and Thoreau, Chekhov and Ibsen, Beethoven and Brahms. The universal values know no frontiers of time or space. Thus it is that for most peoples, the truly great art of all periods, and of all cultures, has strong appeal. This is particularly true of the art of the golden ages, the great creative epochs—the architecture of the Italian Renaissance, the music of Austria and Germany, the paintings of Holland and Flanders, and the novels of England and Russia. World literature (the Bible, *The Arabian Nights*, and the writings of Hans Christian Andersen, Cervantes, Goethe, Shakespeare, Tolstoy) communicates universally, as has been shown by the fact that such works are translated into countless languages and are read by countless peoples. It also explains why a medieval Christian cathedral, a Buddhist temple or an Islamic mosque, the Taj Mahal, the Palace of the Doges, or the Alhambra, should all be venerated by people from every land and culture. If no values were universal, and if none were higher than others, how could this be possible?

It is clear that throughout history the human race has celebrated beauty as a quality that enhances life. Human beings have created this beauty, or sought it out or discovered it by serendipity, both in our own artistic triumphs and in nature's cornucopia. These not only contribute to peak moments, but, as we have seen, represent universal experiences. Are there other functions of art, however, in which all men share? In what other ways do art and aesthetics contribute to the enrichment of human life?

On this point, those who have explored the theory and philosophy of art, John Dewey and Herbert Read in particular, have much to say. Art, they hold, is the great unifying force in all communities and has been perhaps the most enduring element in civilization. As Albert Camus observed, "Man cannot do without beauty."[85] The

---

art which captures this beauty helps us to make sense of the myriad impressions with which we are bombarded in day-to-day living. Art then is more than basic to life; it is the very essence of life. Even though bread be the staff of life, mankind cannot live by bread alone. Without art, individuals become alienated and the human community deteriorates.

Those who are most attuned to the aesthetic, who easily recognize the intrinsic rightness of things, are also those who are healthiest in a psychological sense. Reversing this, there is evidence that psychologically healthy people, wherever they are found and regardless of race, culture or class, not only prefer goodness (i.e. kindness, gentleness, tenderness) over evil, but like trained artists will choose beauty over ugliness. However, it is not only these who are able to perceive beauty. Apparently those whose talent is highly developed in one area, and who may not be self-actualizing, may nevertheless be discriminating in their choices of beauty. Interestingly enough, those with the most highly developed sensibilities—the practicing artists— have been shown in a study by Irvin L. Child to be much more like one another, in their tastes and choices of "preferred art," irrespective of their culture, than they are like nonartists in their own society.[86]

There is considerable agreement that the healthy community and its citizens and artists produce great art. What they celebrate is the drama of life and not pale shadows or hollow echoes—theories of art, grammar or rhetoric. For art is a bond between human beings that conveys the real meaning of ideas and of religion. Through it, as Dewey said, abstractions are "changed from doctrine into living experience."[87] Read contended similarly that "life itself is aesthetic" and that it is a mistake to delineate a world of art and set this apart from life. If we regard art as the ultimate way of teaching, as Shelley did, and can also concede that it works through the imagination—through empathy and love—we begin to see the inseparability of the higher values. "A man to be greatly good must imagine intensely and comprehensively." Edwin Markham expressed this succinctly in his small verse, "Outwitted."

> He drew a circle that shut me out—
> Heretic, rebel, a thing to flout.
> But Love and I had the wit to win:
> We drew a circle that took him in!

Dewey conceived of art as a part of all living, as the heart of being. He expressed his view in the following analogy:

> "Mountain peaks do not float unsupported; they do not even just rest upon the earth. They *are* the earth in one of its manifest operations."[88]

According to him, all people value aesthetic experiences. They relish all manner of things "in part, at least, because of their aesthetic quality." They enjoy watching fires—the great holocaust of the three-alarm as well as the glowing coals of the campfire. They are captivated by life and growth. Midwestern American farmers go out on hot nights to "hear the corn grow"; people record weight gains (at least of babies and children) with delight; householders raise flowers which, with great satisfaction, they watch come into bud and bloom. All peoples have also used decoration in many parts of their lives. Bodies are decorated in a fantastic variety of ways, from sequinned cocktail gowns to well-polished nose rings; and surroundings and tools are decorated and beautified with loving care.

Art is present, Read contends, in all things that men make which "please our senses." All human groups experience this delight in hearing, tasting, smelling, touching. Or in Yeats's words: "Art bids us touch and taste and hear and see the world." Different peoples, however, through predisposition or training, exemplify this universal characteristic in different ways. Thus certain communities may center on a particular type of sensory expression or appreciation. The Japanese, for example, greatly value tactile experiences. The bowls they use in the tea ceremony are artistic creations of the highest order and are particularly valued for their shape and texture. As the tea drinking proceeds, each bowl is handed from one kneeling participant to the next, so that all initiates can not only partake of the fragrance and the taste of the thick green tea, but can also "feel" the bowl. These tea bowls are sometimes covered with high-gloss glaze; but often the most prized among them are irregularly shaped and have a rough clay outer surface.[89]

Students of the Far East recognize that the Japanese prize the natural and all that directly or symbolically expresses nature. Read observes that the "form" which is basic to all the art of all people tends to relate to the elementary forms of nature. It is his conclusion that since nature is always the base, the "formal properties" of art do not vary from country to country or from age to age. He believes that "the touchstone outside the individual peculiarities of human beings . . . is nature." By nature he means "the whole organic process of life and movement which goes on in the universe, a process which includes man, but which is indifferent to his generic idiosyncrasies, his subjective reactions, and temperamental variations." These forms are outer manifestations, but are also aspects of the inward. Art enables the individual to coordinate and give meaning to chaotic impressions so that, as Read says, "experience falls into shape."[90] Beyond this, it unifies the "enduring elements in a civilization."

Throughout history, Dewey claims, art is an enduring element:

" 'The glory that was Greece and the grandeur that was Rome' for most of us . . . sum up those civilizations; glory and grandeur are aesthetic."

It was his view that art expresses the aliveness of an era as well as the quality of its life. In turn, it is the most persuasive teacher. The world over, it serves as a natural, soft-spoken counselor-guide, far more effective than the pedant. To conclude with Dewey's words:

"Art is more moral than moralities. For the latter either are, or tend to become, consecrations of the *status quo*, reflections of custom, re-enforcements of the established order. The moral prophets of humanity have always been poets even though they spoke in free verse or by parable."[91]

CHAPTER FOUR

Evolution of the hierarchy of values—the good person

In the course of their histories, both the concepts expressed in a hierarchy of values and the social institutions which seek to embody them have undergone an evolution which is continuous, although by no means even and consistent. Over the centuries, this evolution has taken the form of an open, upward spiral, embracing in its sweep the two ideals of the good person and the good society. Before these are explored, however, certain preliminary distinctions should be drawn so as to clarify the meaning of a hierarchy of values in relation to change or development.

First, we may distinguish between stages of development simply in terms of the time sequence: something occurs later than something else. No hierarchy is involved in this; nor is any value implied, since no necessary correlation exists between early or late and either good or bad. This should be clear if we consider the value which some persons attach to modernization, on the one hand, or to antiques, on the other. Modernization is sometimes advocated with the implied assumption that the modern way of doing things is the good one and the traditional way is bad, a clear instance of a *non sequitur*. Conversely, there are some who are so enamored of anything old that they may approve it, whether it be useless or ugly or harmful. Novelty, as such, contains no more inherent superiority than does antiquity.

Second, there is a kind of development which consists primarily of a positive change in magnitude, a growth from small to large. This is a process of mere accretion or aggregation, such as heaping stone upon stone. Its effects are quantitative and are measurable on a numerical scale. As with a sequence in time, a change in size, especially in the form of an increase, connotes neither a hierarchy nor a change in value. While it is true that a change in degree can result in a certain change in kind, we should not confuse bigger with better. Frequently, the smaller may be the superior.

A third type of change is from simple to complex. In this case, there is certainly an element of hierarchy, although it is not invariably true that the more complex is superior. Admittedly, if we compare the human brain with that of a bird, the greater complexity of the former is one aspect of our superiority. But certain structures, such as some very big bureaucracies, can grow to the point where their very complexity becomes self-defeating because other qualities (good morale, for example) are normally lost in the process. Moreover, what should we say of a person whose brain has so advanced in complexity that he is able to conceive and construct a thermonuclear bomb? At this particular task, such a brain is superior to those of the majority of its contemporaries and of its ancestors one million years ago. But is its possessor a morally superior person?

The fourth kind of change is qualitative. This is marked by a development from lower values to higher, from inferior to superior. Such a progression implies a ranking, a set of priorities, and therefore a hierarchy among the values themselves. In this case, one distinguishes different stages of development (or types of change) by evaluating them, which means judging some conditions better than others.

As will become clearer when we discuss the evolution and expansion of a hierarchy of values, some of these four aspects of development are at times confused. What appears at first glance to be a hierarchy of values may turn out on closer inspection to be simply a sequence of changes occurring through time, or perhaps an increase in size or complexity. In certain hierarchies, as in some schemes of classification or taxonomy, the value orientation is stated explicitly. In others, values are implied in the examples which are chosen or in the allusions to other work which is manifestly value-oriented. In still other cases, values are ostensibly (or ostentatiously) excluded.

But even where neutrality of judgment is claimed, one will often discover an ordering or selection of the material which corresponds with the values of the writer's culture (for example, the Judeo-Christian ethic is generally influential in Western Europe or North America). And it sometimes happens that a taxonomy, which is labeled neutral by the theoreticians who formulated it, may be used as a scale of values by its practitioners.

Keeping in mind these cautions and distinctions, let us now see how hierarchies of values have been applied to the development both of individuals and of communities.

In search of the good person

Nowhere is the evolution of our values more clearly seen than in the enlarging concept of individual growth, of human potential, of what each of us truly is and might ideally become. Our hierarchies of values have come to reflect the concepts of limitless development and increasing integration. They envisage the actualizing of human potentialities through a dynamic process of stages of development to higher levels, always more complete. Each part (aspect or facet) of the human being may be developed in turn, or several may unfold and grow simultaneously; and each interacts with the others in a constantly expanding whole.

This process can be witnessed as the baby begins to coo and babble, the prelude to speech. Next, the infant may explore walking patterns (during which time the talking does not always progress, but may be stored, as it were, temporarily on a shelf). Having mastered the rudiments of walking, the child may return to talking, which is integrated with walking. Later, it proceeds to the more advanced stages of growth—learning, evaluating, thinking creatively and critically. This aspect of a hierarchy of values—the integrative —is dynamic, and is always in process of becoming. What occurs during the process is not merely a coordination or convergence of acts which, viewed externally, exhibit a pattern of relationships. In a deeper sense, as Jung maintains, the integration takes place subjectively within the human psyche.

The more highly evolved person is human in the fullest and most complete sense. Such a person has the distinctly human characteristics—a respect for life as we know it, a vision of what it might be, a knowledge of self and the knowledge that we can make choices which will affect our own well-being and that of our counterparts, both contemporary and future. Intellectual development is not then crystallized at a skill level, but has proceeded to the point where individuals are thinking about what integrates their own personalities and unites each person with mankind as a whole.

Much more is known today than in earlier times about the human personality and stages of character growth. Many of those who have studied the nature of individual development have charted it as hierarchical, but what supports the apex is not always clear. It is as if all of the mountain except the peak were wreathed with fog. In general, there is much in common between post-World War II research findings on character growth, various hierarchies of self-actualization or ego development, and the kind of positive mental health described by Marie Jahoda.[92] Although these researchers depict the highest level of ego or character development in similar terms, they have different conceptions of what the hierarchy is. Some have traced a developmental sequence and a characterology irrespective of age level. Others have formulated steps which lead to this highest level by observing concrete stages of growth in children.

The stages of development that will be presented here are built from a number of research studies and theoretical statements. It is important to recognize that this kind of grading in successive stages (the developmental sequence) is abstract and therefore somewhat arbitrary. Inevitably, every model is a simplification. However, there is a striking convergence of views as to what is high and what is low, what is superordinate or subordinate. These formulations include hierarchies constructed to represent milestones of ego development (Loevinger[93]), moral stages (Kohlberg[94]), levels of human existence (Graves[95]), character development (Peck and Havighurst[96]), intellectual and creative growth (Drews[97]). Although often derived from field studies, the building of these schemata, as noted above, is formal and primarily cognitive. Kohlberg, Peck and Havighurst, and Drews based their classifications upon observation and research with children and youth. Loevinger, Graves, and—to an extent— Maslow[98] use more purely theoretical constructs. Maslow's highest category, however, the self-actualizing person, is founded on his studies of this group of people.

Not all of the higher order images of humanity, referred to later as levels VI and VII, have been presented with supporting hierarchies. Nevertheless, most of those who discuss or project the various ultimates in human potential, and who sketch out the growth ladders by which the heights are reached, consider that only a few persons attain the higher levels of development. Those, moreover, who regard our species as basically and potentially good or as possessing transcendent qualities, are convinced that the mass of humanity do not begin to approach their attainable pinnacles of personal development. On the qualities of the ideally good person—and the varying degrees to which mankind falls short of the ideal—there is far more similarity than difference between the 20th-century statements of Rogers,[99] Mumford,[100] A. Huxley,[101] de Chardin,[102] Polanyi,[103] and those made throughout the ages by the spokesmen of the great religions and philosophies.

The stages of individual development

Table 1 lists the seven stages of individual development which have been derived from the work of representative theorists and researchers.

Loevinger divides the first stage, Level I, into two—presocial and symbiotic. The presocial (or autistic) stage is one in which the child does not distinguish between animate and inanimate parts of the environment. In the next stage (symbiotic), the child separates the mother, but not the self, from the environment. This is a prelanguage (infancy) stage and seems to correspond to Graves' Reactive Level. At this level, the individual seeks satisfaction of basic physiological needs and puts a high value on the cessation of tension. Infants and mental retardates are generally placed here.

Loevinger describes Level II as an impulse-ridden stage where the child lacks control much of the time, and interpersonal relations are exploitive and dependent. Kohlberg's Stage 1 of his preconventional level probably fits here. It is characterized by unquestioning deference to superior power. Peck and Havighurst describe their amoral character type as what is often called clinically the "psychopathic personality"—a person who gratifies whims and impulses without regard for their effects on others. Graves indicates that his Animistic Stage, although ascribed to primitive people rather than children, is dominated by attempts to manipulate the world to obtain security.

At Level III, Loevinger speaks of an expedient and opportunistic morality. The individual now attempts to get the better of others and to control them. This is much like Peck and Havighurst's Expedient Adolescent and Drews' Social Leader, both of whom seek to manipu-

Table 1

The stages of individual development

Level I   Presocial (Loevinger[93]), Reactive (Graves[95]).

Level II   Impulse-ridden (Loevinger), Animistic (Graves), Pre-conventional, Stage 1 (Kohlberg[94]), Amoral (Peck and Havighurst[96]).

Level III   Opportunistic (Loevinger), Materialistic (Level 4, Graves), Preconventional, Stage 2 (Kohlberg), Expedient (Peck and Havighurst), Social Leader (Drews[97]).

Level IV   Conformist (Loevinger), Ordered existence (Level 3, Graves), Conventional, Stage 3 (Kohlberg), Conforming (Peck and Havighurst), Studious (Drews).

Level V   Conscientious (Loevinger), Belonging (?) (Graves), Conventional, Stage 4 (Kohlberg), Irrational-Conscientious (Peck and Havighurst), Studious (Drews).

Level VI   Autonomous (Loevinger), Personalistic (Graves), Post-conventional, Stage 5 (Kohlberg), Rational-Altruistic (Peck and Havighurst), Creative Intellectual (Drews), Fully Functioning (Rogers[99]), Specialist (Arnold[104]), Productive Personality (Fromm[105]).

Level VII   Integrated (Loevinger), Being-motivated (Graves), Postconventional, Stage 6 (Kohlberg), Gifted Generalist (Arnold), Self-Actualizing (Maslow[98]), World Man (Mumford[100]), Universal Man (de Chardin[102]), Fully Human (Huxley[101]), Arete (Socrates[106]), Cosmic Consciousness (Bucke[107]), Superior Person (Polanyi[103]), Beautiful Person (Jewish, Chinese Traditions[108]).

late and to win by any means. In general, this is a level corresponding to Kohlberg's Stage 2 of the preconventional, in which the individual's main purpose is to satisfy his own needs. "Human relations are viewed like those in the marketplace."[109] Graves seems to reverse the general order by placing his Materialistic, "will to power" stage above the conforming one (Riesman's "tradition-directed man").

At Level IV conformity is the dominant pattern. This has been particularly well documented and is the subject of wide comment and research by psychologists and social scientists. We have the picture of the individual absorbing the color of the group and so internalizing its rules and mores that he normally conforms without thinking about it. Kohlberg speaks of this as the good-girl and good-boy orientation. A person seeks approval by being "nice" and is rewarded accordingly. Drews noted that in the schools it was the studious behavior which was most often lauded by the majority of teachers as well as by administrators.

At Level V morality is wholly internalized. Rather than conform, the individual follows his own conscience and is less apt to respond to group pressures. People at this stage are usually self-critical and guilt-ridden. Peck and Havighurst speak of the blind or rigid superego at work. It is their view that the Irrational Conscientious type demonstrates an alternative form of childlike morality, occurring at the same developmental level as the Conforming type. Loevinger, however, places this level above conformity in the developmental sequence. She points not only to the increase in internalization, but also to a change in interpersonal relations. The latter, as she says, are now "seen in terms of feelings and traits rather than actions; they become more vivid, intensive and meaningful than in the earlier periods."

Level VI is the stage which has been designated as autonomous. The individual has become more self-aware and recognizes many inner conflicts. The search for one's identity is troubled by internal inconsistencies. For Kohlberg, this is the beginning of the postconventional level and is "characterized by a major thrust toward autonomous moral principles which have validity and application apart from the authority of the groups or persons who hold them and apart from the individual's identification with those persons or groups." But in Loevinger's conception, "interpersonal relations remain intense." People at this stage recognize their mutual interdependence as well as the need that each has for autonomy. Drews has stressed the independence of mind which characterized the creative intellectual adolescents she studied, while Peck and Havighurst noted the concern of their Rational-Altruist for "the welfare of others, as well as himself." Both Creative Intellectuals and Rational-Altruists were found to work actively for their principles.

At Level VII, the highest stage, which Loevinger calls integrated, the individual has evolved beyond coping or even beyond creative autonomy to an olympian or cosmic view. Such a person, while remaining responsible, is now also engaged in a "search for meaning." Kohlberg describes his Postconventional level, Stage 6, as a time when the individual makes decisions of conscience and chooses ethical principles which appeal to logical comprehensiveness, universality and consistency. Maslow speaks of the "reconciliation of opposites" achieved by the self-actualizing person. At the highest level of all, some believe, certain rare persons are capable of attaining a transcendental state where, as Blake thought, "everything appears as it really is, Infinite."

As the table indicates, some theorists and researchers have formulated hierarchies which include all of these stages. Both Loevinger and Graves, for example, have seven levels, although they reverse the ranking of Levels III and IV. The former classifies opportunistic behavior as Level III, while the latter's description of this kind of person—Exploitative—comes under his Level IV. Loevinger places Conformist at Level IV whereas Graves assigns a similar phenomenon, Ordered Existence, to Level III. Others have the same completeness of detail, but within a more limited range or age sample. If infants are excluded, one has to omit what Kohlberg calls the Preconventional, Stage 1, and what Loevinger divides into two stages—the Presocial or Autistic, and the Symbiotic. It is the latter's view that "the ego can hardly be said to exist prior to the end of this stage."[110] This first stage appears to resemble Graves's Reactive level where the primary search is for "satisfaction of basic physiological needs."

Neither Drews' Creative Intellectual nor Peck and Havighurst's Rational-Altruist was placed in Level VII, since in both cases their categories were developed in work with adolescents; and, although they could well apply to adults, this was not the intent of these studies. On the other hand, the formulations by Bucke, Arnold, Maslow and others all came about as a result of a study of adults through biographies, observations, or personal acquaintance.

The ways in which individuals reach the apex may vary widely. But when they have attained a very high level of development, there is much similarity in the descriptions of how they appear to others. Likewise, religions and philosophies speculating on the ideal have made closely approximating statements about what the ideal is. In other words, it would appear that at the highest levels of development all of the more superficial differences—age, sex, social class, religious denomination, race, or ethnic group—become unimportant. It is worth noting, however, that those who do the classifying, despite their generosity of outlook, tend to place at the highest level a disproportionately large number of their own kind. Mumford and Emerson, for example, list few who are not white males of the Western civilization. As an ancient Greek once said, if horses had a concept of gods, they would imagine them as hippomorphic.

Kohlberg discusses what he calls "The Final Step," wherein the individual "has disentangled his judgments of—or language about—human life from status and property values (Stage 1), from its uses to others (Stage 2), from interpersonal affection (Stage 3), and so on; he has a means of moral judgment that is universal and impersonal."[111] He says he was told by anthropologists that he would have to learn "a whole new set of values for each new culture," but his research disclosed convergence both in what was valued and in the ways the values were ranked. Social class and religious differences were also found to be relatively unimportant. He reports that "middle-class and working-class children move through the same sequences, but the middle-class children move faster and farther." Further, the sequence did not depend upon a particular religion since the development of morals did not differ significantly, "among Catholics, Protestants, Jews, Buddhists, Moslems and atheists."[112]

To present the stages of individual development in such a schematic form may appear to imply that all individuals invariably proceed through these same stages in the same sequence. In fact, certain researchers have contended that a maturing individual must necessarily pass through all stages of growth in a fixed and predetermined pattern. Thus Piaget, Bruner, and Kohlberg (who modeled his work on Piaget) suggest that mental and moral growth proceed in an orderly progression. "All movement is forward in sequence, and does not skip steps," as Kohlberg states it[113]—although he does allow that children can move through these "true" stages at varying speeds and that an individual's growth may stop at any stage.

Such a view is too rigid to be universally true, for the patterns of individual growth are many and diverse. No two lives, even those of identical twins, exactly replicate one another. The knowledge of individual development which has grown out of other theories and unstructured observation seems to point to other equally valid conclusions. We have already noted Chomsky's assertion that each child has an innate "idea of language" and can use a complex syntax when very young.[114] Is it not possible that some of the young also think at a high level and in complex terms? Moreover, if one believes that a child is naturally good and that it is society and its institutions which corrupt, it would not seem either logical or psychologically necessary to hold that each would follow an "invariant developmental sequence" and go through a "Lord of the Flies" stage.[115] One might instead express brotherly love as a very young child. In other words, if a certain inherent goodness is a characteristic of at least some very young children, all children may not experience all stages. Some will not engage in cruel behavior even when there are "holes in the power structure," to use Kohlberg's phrase.

Nor is it inevitable that all steps be experienced in the same sequence. Psychological or mental health is not the same as physical maturity. It is both conceivable and possible that goodness (including adherence to truth, appreciation of beauty, etc.) in some cases may already be developed in the very young—as Athena in the Greek myth was said to have emerged from the head of Zeus full-grown and clad, or as a child's insights might reveal that it is attuned to what has been called Cosmic Consciousness. In that case, we would not be saying that goodness grows or matures (in the same way, for example, as a growing body can develop muscular strength), but rather that it is uncovered or revealed. Furthermore, that stages may be skipped or that several may be telescoped together is quite evident in the case histories reported by Catherine Cox on the highly gifted—those whom society has designated as geniuses and some of whom the humanistic psychologists would characterize as self-actualizing.[116]

Nevertheless, despite the various interpretations of how an individual fits into (or develops within) a hierarchy, the concept of growth as an upward thrust seems to be uncontested. All do not grow at equal rates, however, nor do all make positive gains throughout their lives. Many may reach an apparent plateau of moral maturity at an early age, e.g. leveling off at an opportunistic, self-centered mode in adolescence, while others may actually regress. Just as societies can regress, slipping backwards from civilization to barbarism, so can individuals. Charlotte Buhler has pointed out how some persons continue to lead lives of creative expansion, while others narrow their vision and their interests.[117] With some, intelligence continues to rise; in others, it appears to decline after physical maturity is reached. Most researchers feel that people improve in moral terms throughout youth. But it is possible that a few deteriorate in character from birth onward and become psychopathic. The child may be naturally good, as Rousseau suggested,[118] but the original nature may be poisoned by harmful influences in the environment.

And just as some adults may undergo genuine conversion and be transformed into saintliness, others may be corrupted and decay within (a possibility which Oscar Wilde treated imaginatively in *The Picture of Dorian Gray*). The point is that human beings do change; and some—for reasons and in ways not fully understood— become more highly developed than others and more truly human. It appears, as Hadley Cantril has stated the proposition, that "both the individual and the species . . . follow an ever-ascending path;"[119] and, possibly, that individual growth moves to the heights more smoothly in the ambience of a good environment.

CHAPTER FIVE

Evolution of the hierarchy of values—the good society

In search of the good society

"At the foot of the rainbow there is a pot of gold." So ran the old folk-saying; and many of the young would set out from their villages in the direction where the rainbow arched across the sky, searching for the spot where it came to earth.

When chemists (or alchemists) in the Middle Ages were seeking an ingredient to convert base metals into gold, the object of their quest was called "the philosopher's stone." Among philosophers, as among their fellowmen, there have been many who imagine a golden age of peace and justice which they contrast with the dismal here and now. But they have been of two minds about where and when to place it. Some have seen the darkness of their contemporary world as the aftermath of a bygone golden noon; others, as the interval before a golden dawn.

What would a good society be like? What should be the values toward which we might direct ourselves? And how can we achieve this ideal community? These are among the eternal questions which humanity has never ceased to ask. Since the quest for a good society is itself aided by ideas about its possible character, we shall consider what some of the leading social thinkers have said on this subject, or have neglected to say. For social development stems ultimately from no impersonal objective forces, but from the visions of the imaginative. As someone has cautioned: "Be careful what you want. You may get it!"

The ideal of the good society cannot be discussed in exactly the same way as that of the good person, because the two concepts have had a different history. On the qualities of the good person, as we noted above, the teachings of the world's major religions and philosophies are similar to the research findings of psychologists who have studied character development. And it is significant that no one has ever suggested a higher goal for the individual human being to aspire to than did Gautama or Jesus. This is another way of saying that the ideal of the Good Person attained a lofty peak at least two thousand years ago and since then has not been raised significantly. The same is not true, however, of the ideal of the good society. Plato, for instance, sketched a utopia, i.e. his notion of a perfect community, in the *Republic*. But that utopia included slavery, preparation for war, and a belief in the permanent division of mankind into unequal classes. Certainly in these respects, all modern utopias represent a considerable change.

Prior to the 20th century, values of one kind or another occupied a central position in all social philosophies in the West. Beyond their agreement on that point, however, the disagreements run deep. What some thinkers rank low in their hierarchy of values, others rank high. Thus, Plato insisted on the virtues of unity and order; Rousseau, on freedom and spontaneity. Locke prized the consent of the governed; while Hobbes preferred the power of the governors. Each of the five images of Man which were discussed in Chapter One has had its exponents and supporters in different times and places; and on the foundations of those images various theories have been constructed about the form which society and its government should take.

Amid so much diversity, however, there are two sets of antithetical values on which we shall focus particular attention, because it is this contrast of view which is basic to an understanding of the ideals of the good person and the good society. Those thinkers who see mankind as good or as potentially transcendental insist on the primacy of the person, whose unique worth is sacred and inviolable. Healthy growth, both of the good person and the good society, would take place from the inside out, leading both to self-realization and to community with others. In the drama of every life, such a concept sees each individual as actor and playwright who seeks to express, through freedom and diversity, the values of truth, beauty, and love. The contrary values are those of thinkers who, because they do not trust humanity, put their trust in the state or in other forms of external authority. The direction for change will then be imparted to the individual from without. In this case, people are puppets, no longer in command of their own destinies. The person does not act, but is acted upon by the surrounding system. The good society, so conceived, is that which exhibits the virtues of order and obedience. Those who succeed on its terms are rewarded with wealth, power, and status.

In the present century, however, another style of thinking has arisen and is the current vogue among those who prefer to consider themselves social scientists rather than social philosophers. The fashion they affect is to avoid evaluation—to be objective in their work and value-free. They have chosen to do this on these professed grounds: that they wish their study of human society to be as scientific as possible, that to be scientific is to base one's findings on data which are objective and external to the viewer, and that values are a subjective judgment which, if introduced into conclusions, will render them unscientific. As we shall argue later, they do not in fact practice what they preach (for the very simple reason that it is impossible). But it is interesting, to say the least, that they should have thought it possible and even valuable to abdicate from value judgments. There is a brief dialogue between Sherlock Holmes and Dr. Watson, in which the master-sleuth remarked to his ever-faithful but dull-witted companion: "Did you notice the unusual incident of the dog in the night?" "But," objected Watson, "the dog did nothing in the night." "That, my dear Watson, was the unusual incident." What is self-revealing about so many social scientists, both recent and contemporary, is what they have ostensibly chosen not to do.

In the pages that follow, we shall first refer to the different value preferences of certain leading figures in the tradition of western political thought. Next, we shall discuss, and evaluate, the so-called "value-free" method of the modern social sciences. The treatment, because brief, will not be complete. But it will serve to point the contrast between three fundamental attitudes relating to values: those who believe that mankind is basically good and that, consequently, a good society is possible; those who see their fellow humans as merely ineffectual or as downright bad and society as a reflection of these traits, and finally, those who claim to be avoiding values altogether, but often tacitly accept the bad ones such as power or status.

Plato was the earliest to develop in a systematic form the notion of an intimate relationship between the character of the community and that of the person who belongs to it. In the *Republic*, he argued that human beings must live virtuously if they are to be happy and that virtue derives from the wisdom which only the rule of reason can ensure. Since few persons are sufficiently endowed with reason, these (the philosopher-kings) must be the ones to govern. The rest will find their happiness in obedience to the supremely wise. Then, as he delineated the imperfect communities which degenerated downward in a hierarchy from the good to utter evil, in each case he also portrayed the psychological characteristics of the accompanying personality.[120] In descending order from the ideal, these were: timocracy (where those who rule are imbued with a code of honor—part aristocratic, part military), oligarchy (the rule of the rich), democracy (the rule of the many dominating the aristocracy and the wealthy), tyranny (the despotism of one who is himself the slave of his passions).

Aristotle fortified his social philosophy with a method for which Plato had neither the interest nor the inclination. He studied and compared the social orders and governmental systems of 158 communities, compared the findings and then proceeded inductively to arrive at generalizations based on the data he had collected and classified. For this reason, he has frequently been cited as the prototype of the empirical researcher. But this overlooks the point that Aristotle combined his inductive method with deductive theorizings about ethics and metaphysics. Not only did he pass value judgments on his data, but he presented in the *Politics* his own philosophy of the ideal citizen in an ideal *Polis*. One cannot applaud Aristotle and simultaneously say: "Values, adieu!"

The breakdown of the *Polis*—which was city, state, and community, all combined in one small package—was followed by the clash of competing empires, each seeking to organize large segments of humanity under its jurisdiction. To these altered circumstances, the response was a great forward leap of the spirit. A universal philosophy (Stoicism) and a universal religion (Christianity) were developed. The Stoics believed that reason permeates the universe and is divine. Since all human beings are endowed with reason, we are basically equal. For, in that which is fundamental to our humanness each of us possesses a spark, however infinitesimal, from the same

Aristotle commences the Politics *as follows: "Every*
state is a community of some kind, and every
community is established with a view of some good;
for mankind always act in order to obtain that
which they think good. But if all communities aim
at some good, the state or political community,
which is the highest of all, and which embraces all the
rest, aims at good in a greater degree than any
other, and at the highest good."

(Translated by Benjamin Jowett, Oxford: Clarendon Press,
rev. ed., 1921.)

---

divine fire. Such an institution as slavery is contrary, therefore, to
nature since the slave has reason and, through this, a share in the
godhead.

The same universal humanity inspired the teachings of Jesus, who
has been called "the greatest communal equalitarian of them all."[121]
Jesus added what the Stoic doctrine had lacked. He suffused reason
with faith; duty, with love. Love was the uniquely Christian message
and it knew no bounds. Beyond the family, it extended to one's
neighbors as well as to enemies. Peace was to be preferred to war;
meekness to power; poverty to wealth.

Like Socrates before him, Jesus was deemed too dangerous by the
power structure of his day and was put to death. But when the religion which his life and crucifixion had inspired had captured the
inner citadel of Roman power, it too suffered the fate of anything
which belongs to the spirit when it is institutionalized. Becoming
incorporated in the system, the Church now planted itself between
humanity and deity, claiming that it alone held the keys to the kingdom. Consequently, such philosophers of Christianity as Augustine
and Aquinas were torn between the faith in which they devoutly believed and the organized authority whose apologists they became.
The former, therefore, introduced the doctrine of the "just war,"
maintaining that Christians are right to do battle against "bar-
barians." The latter proclaimed his hierarchy of law, placing at the
top that which comes from God and at the bottom that which issues
from men. But he neglected to point out that the rules of ecclesiasti-

cal authority are no less man-made than those of the temporal power.

As the medieval Church, especially its wealth and power, deviated more and more from the precepts of the Gospel, voices were raised in protest and action matched the words. The Albigenses and the Waldenses had their own versions of Christianity. These did not coincide with that of Rome, for the direction of their movements was toward purity, poverty and simplicity. Against such threats to its unity, the established order struck back through the persecutions of the Inquisition and with military massacres. But the protests continued none the less. Indeed, in the example of Francis of Assisi they attained a spiritual height which almost equalled that of Jesus himself. Here again was the promise that the good person, who lived a saintly life of self-abnegation and loving service to others, could create the good society.

The revolution in values, which the Renaissance and the Reformation jointly fostered, was accompanied by a new structure of social power. The system of nation-states—whose earliest instances were England, France and Spain—was centralizing the feudal patchwork of loosely knit localities while simultaneously asserting its independence of the universal order to which Papacy and Empire aspired. Along with this came renewed conflicts over the perennial issues of what kind of person and what kind of society are ideal. Would the new system prove superior to the old?

It was in this context that two thinkers, Machiavelli and Hobbes, baldly presented theories about political behavior which had only been obliquely implied in the two preceding millennia. Central to them both was this question: How do you establish and maintain the power which is needed for holding the state together? Machiavelli, arguing that the ends justify the means, advised all rulers to use the strength of the lion and the cunning of the fox as necessary. These, and other extreme passages, have been frequently wrenched out of context, so that *The Prince* became a Devil's Bible to condone any technique, no matter how immoral. Their author has therefore been much admired by those who interpret politics, divorced from ethics, as synonymous with power. But Machiavelli was less narrowly consistent than the Machiavellians. His writings (*The Prince* included) abound with moral judgments, which were more conventional than elevated, on the actions of rulers and ordinary men alike. He was careful to distinguish between republics and monarchies, expressing a clear preference for the former. Not only did he praise the people for being more honest than their rulers (because the latter are oppressors while the former desire only not to be oppressed), but he himself gave service to the Florentine Republic and not to the Medici. The true Machiavelli was a candid reporter of what he had observed, one who stripped the veil of hypocrisy from the popes and princes of his day and age.

Hobbes, by contrast, was clear-cut and uncompromising in his preference for authority over the rights of the person. Seeking to survive during a civil war, he stated the highest value as security and the power which ensures it. If men are not subjected to a common will, their conflicts will destroy them. His conclusion is therefore: obey the powers that be. For when government loses authority the dissolution of society follows.

Such counsels of prudence and conformity did not commend themselves to thousands of his contemporaries. Resistance to orthodoxy, the right to differ, the assertion of the individual conscience, the search for the truth, within the self—these principles were the foundation of many dissenting groups in the 17th century. Diggers and Levellers, Quakers and Shakers, Huguenots and Anabaptists, were early challengers to the omnipotence of Leviathan. To the new power structures their radical critique was about as palatable as that of the Albigenses and Waldenses had been to medieval popes.

During the last three hundred years, this system which was evolving in the middle of the 17th century has strengthened and entrenched itself. To a degree unparalleled in previous history, it has exploited nature to serve its ends and has hardened its control of human activities. All possible techniques, all modes of organization, were combined for this purpose—military strength which ranged over land and sea, then through the air, and finally into space; scientific discovery and technological invention, which were utilized without regard to moral criteria or ethical consequences; an economy whose corporations united capital with "know-how" into a formidable capacity to produce; a political structure which mobilized its citizens through public education, mass media, and the mystique of nationalism; and the eventual union of economic and political power in the form which Charles Reich has labelled "the Corporate State."

The counterpart to this in the realm of ideas has assumed many guises. When society is transformed by revolutionary changes, all major movements in thought must confront the implications, which means necessarily a concern for values. For what else is a revolution but a fresh look at basic assumptions, or in other words, a re-valuation?

Some thinkers prepare the way for fundamental social change by sceptical inquiry into existing institutions; or, as with Voltaire, Carlyle, or Shaw, by satirizing their more ridiculous pretensions. Some undermine the established order by a blend of merciless criticism and moral indignation, as did Marx, offering at the same time a vision of a future utopia. Others, such as Locke or Jefferson, apply their reason to justify a successful revolution and to inculcate a faith in its promise. Others again are the conservative apologists for a *status quo* whose ordered relationships they do not wish to see disturbed. Thus Hamilton, Burke, and Hegel, who distrusted ordinary humanity, reacted to the French Revolution with horror. Admiring the elite, they favored both inequality, with its accompanying law and order, and the power which can uphold vested interests.

One kind of revolution, or revaluation, has had particularly eloquent exponents during the last three centuries and is the most radical. This is the philosophy which, as we stressed earlier, gives primacy to the person and sees each human being as endowed with unlimited capacity to grow from within. A clear example of this is Rousseau, and with him belong such idealists as Wordsworth, Blake, Emerson, and Thoreau. These thinkers have seen the institutions of conventional society—political, ecclesiastical, and economic—as prison walls which confine mankind in predetermined limits and prevent the development of powers which are potentially transcendental. For them, the climax of the revolution—the liberation of the human spirit—has yet to come.

The poverty of social science

Despite their manifold differences, all the philosophies reviewed so far had this in common: They were willing to express openly whatever values they preferred. In the 20th century, however, a style of thinking has emerged whose aim departs, no less openly, from the earlier traditions. Its avowed preference is to avoid value preferences altogether. Describing themselves as social scientists, in order to mark themselves off from social philosophers, such thinkers consider that to be value-free is a criterion of the true scientist. During the five decades from 1920 to 1970, this pattern of research has exerted a powerful influence on every branch of social inquiry. Consequently we must note, when writing about values, what the social scientists set out to do and appraise the results.

Their aim has been to develop a study of mankind and of human society by a method similar to that used by physical scientists. To accomplish this, the social scientists work within a framework of prescribed rules, consisting of "thou shalt" and "thou shalt not." On the permissible side, as empiricists, they observe and record the behavior of people or animals and conduct experiments under controlled conditions wherever possible. The resulting data are then collected and classified, and correlations are traced. Since data can be more easily processed and compared if they are similar in form, social scientists seek to measure their phenomena and express them in terms of quantities. (A quantity can be counted; a quality cannot be.) Hence the predilection for amassing statistics and for using higher mathematics to analyze what the figures disclose. What is not permitted is the introduction of any subjective element into their work. True social scientists do not express value judgments. Moreover, they claim that the values which they personally hold do not enter into their findings, and they further assert that the way the results are used is not their concern.

What have the social scientists accomplished by these methods? To answer this question, we must do what they profess not to do: We shall evaluate the results.

On the positive side, the simple, self-evident gain which has issued from the labors of social science is a great increase in our store of information. Viewed quantitatively, what is now known about human beings, individually and in groups, amounts to a vast extension of knowledge. More has been accumulated in the last twenty-five years than in the previous twenty-five centuries.

But data do not interpret themselves. Quantity is not quality. Knowledge is not wisdom. Nor can we truly see without insight, hear without listening, count without comprehending. The question we have to direct to the social scientists is this: Has your work significantly contributed to the improvement of self-understanding and of human civilization? What Robert S. Lynd inquired has to be asked again of every experimenter and data collector: "Knowledge for what?"[122]

The course which modern social science has traced may be illustrated by examples from a few of the disciplines—such as economics, political science, and psychology (both experimental and social).

Of the several academic fields devoted to the study of human society, none has gone further in the attempt to be a science than economics. This is because the modern scientific method depends so heavily on quantification, and because there are certain features of the economic system (e.g., prices, wages, interest rates, money supply, production) which lend themselves readily to a quantitative treatment. In such materials the statisticians have a field day. More and more, the speculations of economic theory have become a branch of higher mathematics in which the econometricians have taken over.

But that is not all. For measuring the sum total of what the economy achieves, economists have devised a formula which is well adapted to their method. This is the Gross National Product. The computing and adoration of the GNP has now become the economists' sacred rite.

The trouble is not that the economists have failed, but that they have succeeded too well. The GNP has become the measure to which all other criteria are subordinated. And the result is both distortion and over-simplification. Obviously, the GNP, as such, refers only to the goods and services produced and states them only as an amount. In and by itself, it does not express a quality. It does not specify what is produced, whether housing for the poor or missiles for the military. Neither does it refer to the distribution of the product. In fact, it tells us hardly anything about the values that make the good life. But the use of this particular yardstick contains a hidden implication, a concealed value judgment, which the economists readily embrace. They generally take for granted that it is good for the GNP to increase. More means better; the bigger the quantity, the better the quality. Hence, a country congratulates itself whenever its GNP goes up, and people are urged to work harder and produce more goods whenever it goes down.

That values are, after all, implicit in an allegedly scientific method, and that these values may turn out to be bad, is the reasoning of Scott Paradise in a cogent critique of what he calls "The Vandal Ideology." Analyzing the underlying values of contemporary American society, he writes:

"Since life's primary purpose is producing and consuming, abundant life blesses us through increasing material abundance. Goods equal the good, and nothing can quench our infinite thirst for them. . . . The growth of the GNP does not necessarily lead to the enlargement of human well being. It may in some instances lead to the opposite."[123]

The aberrations of the economists may perhaps be explained in terms of the criticism which Wesley Mitchell, an economist, levelled at his own fraternity half a century ago.[124] Economic theory, he pointed out, was founded on certain assumptions concerning the behavior of human beings, and these assumptions were invariably drawn from a psychology of crude hedonism. The moral: If economics was to become a science of the techniques which will validly fulfill human wants, it must equip itself with a psychology more consonant with the truth. If economic man is a vulgar caricature, calculations based on his supposed behavior are the merest fictions.

In essentials, to the extent that the study of government permits, the political scientists have followed a parallel path. As twin brother to economic man, they invented a political man. They proceeded to endow him with a psychology which equally distorts the reality. They, too, have sought to quantify their data, both where this is a reasonable thing to do and where it is not. And similarly, while professing to be value-free, their studies turn out to be laden with values —often with bad ones.

Political man on close inspection is an old acquaintance. He is the first of the five images which we discussed at the beginning of this work. This is the Hobbesian picture of a human being—insecure, suspicious, aggressive and treacherous. In the economy, he seeks wealth; in politics, he is out for power, hoping through power over others to make himself secure. A political science so conceived is then founded on a conflict model, where hostility and war are represented as natural and normal. Since anarchy (literally, the absence of government) is dangerous, governments must be maintained to enforce peace through domination. System-maintenance and stability are therefore virtues—in other words, values.

On these points, let us cite some representative statements. The identification of politics with power was restated during the era of Hitler, Stalin and Mussolini by Harold D. Lasswell, who leaned heavily on Freud. "Politics," he affirmed, "is the study of influence and the influential. The influential are those who get the most of what there is to get."[125] David Easton has defined the function of the political system as "the authoritative allocation of values." In his view: "The primary goal of political analysis is to understand how political systems manage to persist through time."[126] And finally, there is this interpretation of politics in a recent work by three political scientists:

"One way to begin the study of conflict is to understand that without conflict there is no politics. If everybody decided to quit fighting and always cooperate, the political scientists would be put out of business."[127]

Are the other sciences of human behavior more deeply concerned with real human beings than economics and political science? Take psychology, for instance. Do psychologists see the person whole? The answer must be: not always. Freud, as we have seen, is said to have mainly studied the "sick half." Behaviorists also have generally depicted people as bundles of reflexes, as "hollow men" with nothing inside. Fortunately, another kind of psychology came to the fore in post-war years—the "third force." These psychologists see all persons as being essentially good or transcendent and as having the capacity to live a life both rewarding and beautiful.

But if psychologists, perhaps more than other social scientists, have known that it was possible for man to grow toward the highest possibilities of the human spirit, they too have done things which have harmed individuals directly. Following the leads of Pavlov, Watson, and Skinner, they have experimented directly with people and animals. These scientific studies have in many cases caused psychological or physical damage. School children and psychiatric patients are favorite subjects for conditioning and controlling, along with flat worms, white rats, dogs, pigeons and chimpanzess. Pigeons have often learned such harmless activities as ping-pong. But in one much publicized study, baby chimpanzees were denied their mothers, were given substitutes of wire or terrycloth, and became hopeless neurotics. In another instance, an electric cattle prod was used to condition a child to prevent him from chewing himself. There are innumerable cases where animals are maimed, lobotomized, or killed as part of scientific experiments, and in some reported experiments this has happened to human "patients."[128]

Psychologists, not unnaturally, have become increasingly critical of such practices within their profession. Thus, Julius Seeman wrote an article on "Deception in Psychological Research" in the *American Psychologist*, the official journal of the American Psychological Association.[129] Not only does he speak about the frequency of the use of deception, but he also examines the public policy issues and the ethics involved. He compared the total published literature in several psychological journals for the years 1948 and 1963. Interestingly enough, experimental and clinical journals did not report as many deception studies as did journals of personal and social psychology. These latter showed a great rise in deception. For example, an examination of the *Journal of Personality* and the *Journal of Abnormal and Social Psychology* combined showed 18.5 per cent of such studies in 1948 and 38 per cent in 1963.

What rights, Seeman asks, does the individual have? He maintains that a process which uses deceptive means cannot have a "good" end, and he strongly condemns what he calls "noxious deception." Three cases of unethical side-effects are cited. Two of these involved psychiatric patients who were already seeking mental therapy. One consisted of a group of patients who initially reported high self-esteem and felt that they were highly esteemed by their nurses. They were told, however, that their nurses—who, in fact, had made no ratings—held them in low esteem and they were never subsequently informed of the deception. The other group of psychiatric patients were chosen because they rated themselves as less hostile than most patients. They were then given false profiles showing them to be more hostile than average. Again they were not told they had been deceived. The final study involved a group of randomly selected college men who were told, falsely, that they were latent homosexuals and were never informed otherwise.

Seeman comments that some deceptions, in the name of science, may have irreversible consequences. They can be, as he says, "anti-therapy." He asks that psychologists reexamine their basic assumptions. The primary goal of a discipline, he affirms should not be to accumulate knowledge, but to seek wisdom: "The existence of Hiroshima . . . demonstrates that knowledge alone is not enough. . . ."

These tendencies which we have cited from economics, political science, and psychology, could be illustrated many times over from recent work in these three fields, as well as from sociology and, to a lesser extent, anthropology. The product of modern social science is exactly what could be expected from its initial assumptions. When you start with the notion that subject and object can and should be sharply separated, and that a science must rigidly restrict itself to the objective, you are committed to a false premise which vitiates everything that follows. The social scientists have set themselves a goal which it is impossible to attain. For we can no more understand the world without value judgments than we can live without breathing. Seeking to be empirical researchers, the social scientists try to extract from the totality of everyday experience those phenomena which they can measure, compare and classify. But, as Thoreau has said, "There is no such thing as pure *objective* observation . . ."[130] Polanyi has made it abundantly clear in *Personal Knowledge* that the observer's own choices inevitably enter into and are merged with what is observed. One cannot even begin to collect data without some preliminary definition of what to include and exclude. No affirmative statement is possible unless some matters are emphasized at the expense of others. The scientific practitioners, therefore, necessarily make subjective decisions in which value judgments are intertwined.

However much they pretend to be value-free, in actuality the social scientists belie their own pretensions. But their claims have trapped them in the web of their own make-believe. In pursuing what Theodore Roszak aptly calls "the myth of objective consciousness,"[131] they commit one or the other of two kinds of error, each grounded in a fiction. One of these is the error of reductionism. This means taking the whole reality—the human being, for example, or human society—and arbitrarily subdividing it into segments for study. Because the segments are then isolated from the rest, they are seen in exaggerated form. The result is equally misleading and dehumanizing. It is the method of systems analysis, which seeks to interpret phenomena as subaspects or parts which function within a general system. The latter is then conceived in abstract terms, drawing on metaphors from the stage or the machine. People are presented as actors; their lives are called roles; a design for living is a scenario. Like a computer, the social system absorbs their demands as inputs, processes them, and disgorges its outputs to yield them satisfaction. In this thinking, it is the system which acquires true meaning, as well as life and personality. The human beings, who are processed by it, lose theirs. Of course, any system seeks to maintain itself and defend its boundaries from other systems. Its prime goals, therefore, are stability and survival. Since these are obviously good for the system, they are values.

Whatever this social science may be, very clearly it is value-laden, not value-free. Moreover, the values on which it has preferred to focus are inferior ones. The reductionist who attributes political or economic behavior to the properties of a fictional political or economic man is, of course, taking certain values for granted (e.g. competition or conflict, wealth or power, status or security). Likewise, the systems analyst ordinarily winds up as an exponent of the essential features of the *status quo*. The professed neutrality of the social scientist terminates in partisanship ill-concealed under the robe of objectivity.

The consequences which flow from this way of thinking and acting lie all around us. Just as the majority of physical scientists have come to terms with the established institutions and have conformed to the power they wield, so have thousands of social scientists devoted their abilities to describing or defending the conventional structure. "I maintain strict political neutrality," "How my data are used is not my concern," "I was only following orders"—these attitudes have been a mask for tacit acquiescence or active cooperation in all manner of activities which do not promote human betterment or are harmful to living things. Thus we have seen the earth ruthlessly denuded and disembowelled, rivers and oceans polluted, and the air poisoned. Managers, specialists, technicians, and scientists have worked for their political leaders in extermination camps, as they have abetted the invasion of Czechoslovakia and the destruction of Vietnam. The governments of the two most powerful peoples in the world have deliberately chosen to apply enormous resources of skill and money on voyages to the moon when millions of human beings under their jurisdiction were still living in squalor. As Christians and Muslims, Catholics and Protestants, slaughtered one another in earlier centuries, so in ours have Jews, Buddhists, Confucianists, capitalists, or Communists been identified as "the enemy" in societies which were confused and insecure about their values. Some modern societies have already advanced into moral nihilism.

But that is not all. Over and above these starkly vivid manifestations of stupidity, insanity, or evil, there are other deadly sins which have been infecting the body social, but which are less dramatically visible. Much is written nowadays on the subject of alienation, the feeling on the part of the individual that he or she no longer belongs to the surrounding social order or can identify with it. What causes this? What does it do to a person?

In the modern world, there is another kind of death besides that which is sudden and violent. It is the death of the spirit. It happens to millions that the spirit dies while the body goes on living. They become hollow people, eviscerated hulks, who go through the outward forms and motions of life from which the inner meaning has departed. These are human beings who are stifled by work which so

Individuals can find the security and protection that are prerequisites for freedom only in association with others—and then the organization these associations take on, as a measure of securing their efficiency, limits the freedom of those who have entered into them. . . . We have now a kind of molluscan organization, soft individuals within and a hard constrictive shell without.

John Dewey, *Freedom and Culture, op. cit.,* p. 166.

---

often is routine, repetitive and soul-destroying, and who die slowly from the rage or despair within. They feel oppressed by the weight of the social system, imprisoned by its confining organizations, helpless in the face of its solidity and power. The rewards or satisfactions which they are offered (by the advertising agencies and the commercial television) are crudely materialistic. The body is asked to consume, but the soul is starved. People then develop into the products of a culture which sees the person as serving the system, instead of the other way round. If they are middle-aged or elderly, they are usually so far conditioned that they no longer protest. But if they are young, they explode with anger. And this anger is directed against an education which is designed to create not individuals but conformists; against an economy which no longer satisfies wants but stimulates them; against a machinery of government which appears rigid, remote, unresponsive, and—all too often—corrupt; against the antihuman tendencies of an entire civilization.

Education, as the students see it, is not designed to teach them to think critically, or to evaluate issues in terms of ethical implications. In the public schools they still learn about the great moral ideas of the 18th century: the equal worth and rights of all human beings. But they find themselves shaped as identical items on an endless conveyor belt. They are taught to sit still, to learn what they are told, and to march in and out of the classroom at the dictates of a bell. The university is little better. Frequently the students who memorize what the professor or textbook says receive better grades, more rewards, and often better jobs than those who raise questions or find their own sources. Increasingly, students feel pushed around and without power over their own lives. All about them, they see large problems—poverty, hunger, squalor, prejudice—but institutions of higher education which seem reluctant to be involved with such higher values as justice and love. Instead, many students have found their universities, and some members of the faculty, involved in one way or another, in the management and prosecution of the war in Vietnam. Yet numerous teachers and critics have raised these very questions, often before the students did.

Students, particularly the most able, do not willingly capitulate to the system. Only years of devotion to what some are coming to see as the alienating process of technical scholarship accomplishes this in any final way. We have noted earlier that in their data-collecting and experiments the social scientists try to be objective and per-sonally uninvolved. Their training in the scientist's operational pro-cedures, requires that they not express their most human qualities. They are warned not to sympathize with their human subjects or make friends with their laboratory animals. Such attitudes have also invaded the schools. Supervisors try to be scientific and are called clinical professors. Young teachers are told that routine and disci-pline come before feeling—in some administrations, the beginning student teacher is even cautioned "not to smile before November." In no case are true scientists supposed to be empathically and lov-ingly involved with the people whom they study and with whom they work. Thus scientists are called on to sacrifice their subjective selves, their inner feelings, finally even their personal lives, in order to do things as mechanically, objectively, and as routinely as a machine. As a result, they may become, in Mumford's words "unlov-able and incapable of surrendering to love."[132]

By neglecting to criticize either the effects of the methods they used or the kind of culture which their research buttressed, many value-free scientists worked against the higher values of human beings and the natural world. The human need for self-expression and self-transformation—to reach for something higher and better—was stifled. The needs of the spirit in ethics, aesthetics, religion and critical inquiry were disavowed. The need for intimate association in small, egalitarian groups was displaced by the size and arrogance of huge organizations, both private and public. Not only has the resulting dehumanization been deep and far-reaching, but among its first victims were those who prided themselves on planning or run-ning the system. More than a century ago, Auguste Comte wrote these words which are supremely relevant to our time:

"If we have been accustomed to deplore the spectacle, among the artisan class, of a workman occupied during his whole life in nothing but making knife handles or pinheads, we may find something quite as lamentable in the intellectual class, in the exclusive employment of the human brain in resolving equations or classifying insects. The moral effect is, unhappily, analogous in the two cases. It occasions a miserable indifference about the general course of human affairs as long as there are equations to resolve or pins to manufacture."[133]

Fortunately, however, not all social scientists have succumbed to a way of thinking that reduces their ability to think critically and to raise ethical questions about the results of what they do. Some have deliberately chosen to conduct studies that will make the needs of the poor dramatically clear, while others have used experimental funds to develop new teaching methods which will cultivate curiosity and diversity of thought. Many of the younger social scientists are demanding nowadays that their professional colleagues take action against social wrongs, that they assume moral and social responsibility. They feel that humane concerns must take precedence over scientific methods. They ask that professional groups take political stands, since neutrality, as they say, implies support for the values and policies of the power structure. If you accept money from a corporation or the government and proceed to do what the organization wants done, you are in fact giving your assent to its actions. Thus, your research is inevitably entwined with moral and political issues. Everyone, therefore, must ask: What is the purpose of research? How will it be used? What are its consequences? Whom does it benefit? Whom does it harm?

These, of course, are questions of value. Those who raise them sound less like conventional social scientists and more like social philosophers. What Horace wrote about nature applies just as strongly to the subject of values: "Though you cast nature out with a pitchfork, always it will come running back."

The wealth of social thought

By philosophy we mean reflecting on knowledge, in contrast to the work of 20th-century social science which so often restricts itself to adding to knowledge. Those modern social philosophers with whom we are concerned truly reflect upon knowledge in humanistic and democratic ways. They are, in a sense, romantics who seek to find where the rainbow descends to earth. Assigning the primacy to the growth of the person, not of the system, they believe in the basic goodness of each individual, and are therefore optimistic about the future of the human condition. This distinguishes them equally from those social thinkers whose primary value is to maintain the power of the system and from those whose claim to be value-free and scientifically neutral also results in condoning the values of established power.

Many examples could be cited of 20th-century thinkers, generalists as well as specialists, who have taken this broad and hopeful view of mankind. The list which follows is illustrative only, and is far from being exhaustive: Morris Ginsberg, Pitirim Sorokin, and C. Wright Mills in sociology; Ruth Benedict, Alfred Kroeber, Robert Redfield, Claude Lévi-Strauss, and Margaret Mead in anthropology; Kenneth Boulding, Barbara Ward, the Myrdals, and J. K. Galbraith in economics; Ernest Barker and Carl Friedrich in political science; Teilhard de Chardin and Loren Eiseley in paleontology; Rachel Carson, N. J. Berrill, and Catherine Roberts in biology; Alfred N. Whitehead, Michael Polanyi, René Dubos, and John Platt in physical science; Abraham Maslow and Carl Rogers in psychology; Erich Fromm and Carl Jung in psychoanalysis; and Aldous Huxley, Lewis Mumford, and Arnold Toynbee in the philosophy and history of civilization. These figures with established reputations have been followed more recently by Ernest Becker, Noam Chomsky, Paul Goodman, Michael Harrington, Ronald Laing, Donald Michael, Charles Reich, Theodore Roszak, and Robert Theobald. Such thinkers have wanted to see mankind humanized, not systematized; they have asked not only how people live, but also whether their lives might be happier and better.

In seeking a better way for men to live, the social philosophers continue to be stern critics of society in the tradition of Emerson and Thoreau. Like those 19th-century transcendentalists and mystics, they feel a reverence for all of life. They bring the East and West together as a basis for modern culture. They have used the new insights of those social theorists who help us understand what we are, what ideals we must strive for, and what keeps us from realizing them. Theirs is a robust faith that mankind can come closer in reality to the ideals of the good person and the good society. Similarly, for those who sketch out the life styles of utopias, (such as Lewis

Mumford or Aldous Huxley in *Island*) the good is realizable, not chimeric. They are philosopher-generalists whose range is all knowledge, but they do not disdain the contributions of specialists. In fact, many of them began in an academic specialty or as empirical researchers and then moved from the narrow, partial, and specific to the broad, holistic, and general. These are thinkers who believe that the conventional presuppositions of science are often limited or even false and seek other ways to look at knowledge, society, and the person. Their goal, as Matthew Arnold said of the Greeks, is "to see life steadily and see it whole." Placing the growth of the individual ahead of the survival or stability of the system, they object to that image which depicts human beings as mechanized robots programmed to perform a predetermined role.

Like many of today's youth, the goal they seek is transcendental liberation—personal and communal. They do not give their lives over to the production of things. Theirs is the contemplative attitude in which art, myth and thought combine as a trinity. They speak of a need for a new society with a new way of life. Some say unequivocally with Maslow: "A new vision is emerging of the possibilities of man and of his destiny . . ."[134] Or with Reich: "We are entering a new age of man . . . creating a way of life which is better for human beings."[135] They ask how to be an individual, without being individualistic; how to seek for self, without being self-seeking. The plea of Noam Chomsky for "The Responsibility of Intellectuals," or of Catherine Roberts for "The Scientific Conscience," evokes their immediate response. For with them the individual consciousness embraces a social conscience. They ask that we become aware of ourselves and of the direction our lives are taking, that we recognize and resist the social pressures that control us. It was Thoreau's judgment that "men will be saved when they can be persuaded to desire salvation."[136]

CHAPTER SIX

The history of hierarchies: changing priorities

In the good society, the highest value would be the primacy of the person. The good person is one whose inner growth is aimed at actualizing the highest values—truth, beauty, and love. Synergy, to borrow a term from Benedict and Maslow,[137] is the harmonious interaction of the Good Person with the Good Society. In this chapter we shall attempt to clarify that relationship further, since it has various facets. Ideally, both society and the persons who compose it are conceived as growing; their growth is continuous; a balance is maintained between personal growth and social growth, so that they are reciprocal and mutually reinforcing; the result is integration. Stated negatively, integration could spell an absence of the exceptional and the subjective. The smoothly functioning, cybernated society is an example. Positive integration, however, signifies that the needs and potentialities of the person are at one with the demands and conditions of society.

Our social practice and the broad patterns of our intellectual history have fallen far short of the ideal. In certain particulars, they have even been its direct antithesis. Two points will make this clear. It has been the exception rather than the rule, at least in the western tradition, to insist that personal growth is the prime need of everyone and is also the prime purpose for which our social institutions exist. By contrast, however, great emphasis has been placed in some philosophies on a view of the individual which is extended into a concept of individualism—a doctrine which sees human beings not only as independent, but also as isolable and separate. The relation between such an individual and others is then viewed as an external, virtually mechanical, adjustment to the prevailing system. An individual's success or failure is judged by his or her performance according to its demands, not by the criterion of one's own inner needs and potential. Nothing could be more different from the mystic, from those whom Aldous Huxley called the contemplative. Human beings who lead the inner life can not only become self-aware, but can in the religious sense "transform themselves," and in the metaphysical sense "transcend themselves."

The other respect in which our priorities and practices have departed from the ideal is the failure to arrive at a balanced conception of the person and the society and, consequently, a harmonious integration of both kinds of growth—the personal and the social. Instead, the winds of thought, like the currents of society, have veered in the direction of one pole or another—toward an exaggerated individualism or an equally excessive collectivism. Synergy, whether in doctrine or in deed, has been a rarity.

In the light of these themes, let us now review some further aspects of the history of values and their hierarchies.

The assertion of the self and the loss of community

The modern emphasis on individualism is a result of the revolution in values which occurred in the 16th century when the medieval cast of thought and its attendant feudal order were dissolved in the corrosive acids of the Renaissance and Reformation. Before then, almost all the philosophies of the West had viewed the group as more important than the individual. Both to Plato and Aristotle, a person was a *polites*, a member of a *Polis* (the city-state-community), and all were considered organically interdependent. There is a much quoted statement of Aristotle which is usually translated: "Man is by nature a political animal." But the meaning really is: "Human beings are creatures who can only grow to this full nature in community with their fellows." No word in ancient literature has the meaning that individual has in modern English—save possibly when the antithesis between public and private was drawn. And the Greek for the latter, idiotes, was stigmatized by Pericles in his Funeral Oration as "useless" and in modern usage has degenerated into "idiot."[138]

The principal exceptions to that generalization, as we have seen, were the Stoic teachings and the Christian religion in its original version which Jesus preached. But Stoicism was later corrupted by the power of Rome, as was the Gospel by the power of the Papacy.

Medieval philosophers went along with their Greek predecessors in affirming the organic concept of group membership. What they added was a theological outercoating, as in the Thomist *Summa Theologica*. The medieval artist seldom signed his work; he performed it as a member of his group and for the glory of God. As a human being, he was a mere speck in the cosmos—a creature of the divine creation. Theology saw the individual as a part of a hierarchical order forever bound together in the great chain of ascending values. These led ultimately to the throne of God.

The age of Copernicus and Galileo, of Machiavelli and Leonardo, of Luther and Zwingli, reversed the priorities and produced a new image of mankind. In the new hierarchy of values which emerged, individual achievement was placed at the apex. Individuals were judged to succeed or fail according to the power or status or wealth which they managed to acquire by their personal exertions. That is to say, the criterion for valuation was not the inner development of a person's qualities, but self-aggrandizement on a materialistic scale. On such a scale, the simplest of all measures of worth was money. Everybody could earn this by working for it. Work would bring profit; profit could be saved; savings would accumulate into capital; capital would yield position and power. Society ceased to inquire: "What shall it profit a man if he gain the whole world and lose his own soul?" It preferred to develop the principles of double-entry bookkeeping.

When the individual was regarded, in this individualistic sense, as the natural or proper unit, what happened to society? How, one may ask, was the social good promoted? The answer is that society was now conceived as something artificial, as a work of art which had to be designed and constructed by deliberate human effort. To live in association with one's fellowmen was to be a unit within an aggregate of individuals who had come together by voluntary choice —and could withdraw, if they chose. The whole purpose of the social contract theory in Hobbes, Locke, and Rousseau (although each of them used it to justify a different conclusion) was to explain how and why a group of autonomous individuals could be associated.

The revolution in priorities which the new status of the individual affirmed was judged favorably, on the whole, by the Swiss historian, Jakob Burckhardt when he wrote *The Civilization of the Renaissance in Italy*. In it he saw the occasion for a great outpouring of creative talent previously restrained by the fetters of authority and convention. On the other hand, the British economic historian, R. H. Tawney, is keenly aware that some of the gains made by the individual were losses for society.[139] Mumford supports the latter position, further arguing that some of the values lost were not only in sense of community but also in inwardness and subjectiveness. As a result, the individual was isolated both from himself and from the group, and thus the door was opened for a "capacity for violence, brutality, deviltry." In summary, "The unfettered individual was less of a man than the man of Middles Ages."[140] Arthur Morgan, writing on the small community, agrees that it has been largely destroyed, but maintains that there are traces or remnants which have survived into the 20th century and which can be built upon.[141]

At the end of the 18th century, the faith in the individual was reinforced by an optimistic belief in progress. Two great revolutions, the French and the American, developed their formulations of the rights of all human beings. True, the rights of slaves and women were barely considered worth struggling for, but the great premises were laid down so that the interpretations and subsequent applications could begin. One of the most hopeful and influential advocates of these dreams of the idea of progress was Condorcet.[142] In his *Sketch of a Historical Picture of the Progress of the Human Mind*, which he wrote in prison under sentence of death, he saw ahead to a better future when all mankind would enjoy freedom, equality, and peace. He dreamed of a Utopia that might eventually be realized, of a time when the sun would shine "on an earth of none but freemen, with no master save reason; for tyrants and slaves, priests and their stupid or hypocritical tools, will all have disappeared."[143] Reflecting about the nature of this progress and its direction, how could the human species, he asked, advance "towards truth or happiness?" His answer was to take the progress of knowledge (i.e., Enlightenment) as basic to all other progress. In common with the Encyclopaedists, he held that social institutions were oppressive. Not only was slavery an acknowledged evil, but his vision of a new order extended further to the abolition of war and the equality of the sexes. Finally, because there are no superior or inferior races, this equality should embrace all people on earth.

In this optimistic vision, Condorcet was not alone. Many philosophers in the 18th century considered that humanity could improve and was, indeed, improving. Even the skeptical Hume felt that the human lot in that century was better than in the ancient world. It was at this time that Jefferson was developing a social philosophy and contributing to political action. Declaring that all men are created equal, he maintained that all are endowed with the same fundamental rights. Moreover, he acted on his belief and brought about substantial legal changes in this direction through political means. His goal was to extend the opportunity for education to "the whole mass of the people." Each person, according to his philosophy, has the rights to life, liberty and the pursuit of happiness. Each one of us is able to distinguish right from wrong and is morally inclined to choose the former.[144] Thus in order to have a stable government, every society must examine and choose an ethics of behavior. In other words, it must reach a moral consensus.

Along with this conviction that all persons are basically equal, Jefferson also recognized that there are functional inequalities—in the sense that individuals differ vastly in virtue and intelligence. He voiced no active concern for the rights of women; and, in one letter where he discussed their education, did so in a manner which indicated that women should have a position subordinate to men. Likewise, although he condemned slavery, he was not convinced that members of different races have the same capacities. Arguing the need for leadership, he felt that, if there were free public education, a natural aristocracy—so essential for representative government—would emerge. Although, like most Americans, he had more reservations about human progress than the European philosophers of the Enlightenment, he never doubted that mankind could and would improve. Unlike Condorcet, he thought that laws and institutions could be conducive to good. Because of his fundamental faith in the common man, Hamilton and Adams saw him in his day as a radical. And in some ways, he still is, since many present-day writers do not share the Jeffersonian faith in humanity's natural goodness and capacity for development. However, there are contemporary theorists of human potentiality who go far beyond the ideas which Jefferson voiced.

In the early 19th century, although advances were made in the philosophical groundwork, the main achievement was to open doors for human growth which had hitherto been closed. By mid-century, people were actively demanding that the concepts of democracy be put into effect. In the words of Walt Whitman:

*This last is the most certain, and the most legitimate
engine of government. Educate and inform the
whole mass of the people. Enable them to see that
it is to their interest to preserve peace and order,
and they will preserve them. And it requires no very
high degree of education to convince them of this.
They are the only sure reliance for the preservation
of our liberty.*

Thomas Jefferson to James Madison, in a letter from Paris
dated December 20, 1787 (printed in Koch and Peden, eds.,
op. cit., p. 440).

"I speak the pass-word primeval, I give the sign of democracy. By God! I will accept nothing which all cannot have their counterpart of on the same terms."

Statements of direction, based on formulations of values, were being drafted ever more explicitly. Emerson in America, von Humboldt in Germany, Mill in Great Britain, wrote of self-reliance and liberty and the free development of individuality. Widely read at the time, their essays still serve as an inspiration for democratic thought. Thoreau, a mystic and a radical, made Emerson's dictum, that we should save on the low levels and spend on the high ones, vividly clear by his personal experiment with a new life-style in which he tried to meet the "expectations of the land." Also translating their ideas into conduct, such zealots as John Brown drove their points home by militant actions.

The works of Emerson, who was considered so radical as to be dismissed from his pulpit, were widely respected by many of the leading thinkers of his age, in Europe as well as in America.[145] In addition, via the lecture circuit, his influence reached the general public. A scrubwoman who always attended his lectures in Concord, when asked if she understood him, responded: "Not a word, but I like to go and see him stand up there and look as though he thought everyone was as good as he was."

In fundamental ways, the ideas of this gentle, scholarly man departed from the doctrines generally held at his time. He spoke of the power of thought and will, of inspiration and miracles. Keenly aware of the faults of American society in his day, he was critical of the lack of courage which most people displayed. "We are afraid of truth," he said, "afraid of fortune, afraid of death, and afraid of each other." Yet he felt that mankind, and especially the exceptional individuals, could rise above all this by indomitable spirit, what he called the *vital force.* "Nothing great or new was ever achieved without enthusiasm." Time and time again, he revealed his strong belief in the innate goodness of humanity. Under his influence, religion itself moved in the direction of becoming more naturalized and democratic. He had been appalled by Newtonian physics and by Locke's psychology of "sensation." In the mechanical, materialistic world of such hypotheses, people would be the hapless victims of circumstance, the prisoners of an iron-clad, deterministic universe.

To the American concept of self-reliance, Emerson provided a great momentum. "Whoso would be a man, must be a nonconformist." He vowed not to let the old shibboleths of the past stand in the way of his "being and becoming." The doctrine of Transcendentalism, as interpreted by Emerson, was known as "the party of the Future," and was based on growth and renewal rather than on fixity; and in his writings he laid the groundwork for social reforms and psychological insights which would make it possible for people to be more truly themselves. John Dewey, who ranked Emerson with Plato as one of the world's great moral philosophers, was seeking at the beginning of the 20th century to apply Emersonian ideas in a laboratory school.

Emerson did not shrink from condemning the social order or the orders of his government when they flouted human morality. Persuaded by friends, and after an initial reluctance, he approved of suffrage for women. He also spoke out against slavery with vigor, criticized Daniel Webster for supporting the Fugitive Slave Law, and exclaimed: "I will not obey it, by God!"

But if there was a man whose whole life in fact was the personification of a principle, it was Thoreau. Fourteen years younger than Emerson, Thoreau was greatly influenced by the older man.[146] As a Harvard senior, he read Emerson's first book, *Nature,* and almost immediately there was a shift in the way he saw the world. In an age when few minds had yet grasped the concept of ecology, both of these men had the profound respect for nature which justifies our calling them ecologists. It was through nature, said Thoreau, that we could reach "a higher state of culture." For him, life in the woods and fields was an escape into reality, not away from it. In the mind of the universe all of us share.

With his strikingly original mind and his philosophical insights, Thoreau could well serve as mentor for the new age, as a creator of a better way to live. Beyond merely reflecting on the natural world, he lived intimately with it. It was these observations, particularly during the two years he spent in the frame house he had built on Walden Pond, that formed the basis of his great book, *Walden*. This is one of the very few American works to have won international recognition as a masterpiece and is further distinguished by being a 19th century classic that is still widely read. In it he tells about his intensive observation of the plants, animals, and natural phenomena all about him and reflects on the state of the world. Thoreau found Walden "more favorable, not only to thought, but serious reading, than a university." It served as his retreat, a base where he could practise meditation. One returned to nature to become more cultivated and civilized. Walden supplied the "broad margin" he wanted in his life—time for long conversations, for observations, for appointments with trees, for inspecting snowstorms, for meditations—"which convinced him that he knew what the Orientals meant by contemplation and the forsaking of works."

By concentrating on the how of living and not the wherewithal, Thoreau lived joyfully and serenely. In contrast, as he saw his contemporaries, "The mass of men lead lives of quiet desperation. What is called resignation is confirmed desperation." He spoke of the penance men do "in a thousand remarkable ways" for their possessions, and was scornful of those who sacrifice themselves for things they do not really want.

Many social crusaders and political leaders have based their programs on the principles Thoreau set down. Gandhi read his essay, "Civil Disobedience," as did Martin Luther King. Others find that he shows us the way to live on a higher plane. He studied the New Testament as well as the Eastern mystics and was a confirmed ecumenicist. By beginning "with wildness," and leading an austere and gentle life, one can arrive at transcendental insights into one's innermost self and the "higher laws" of the universe. His dominant mood was that of joy, which he often expressed in an Emersonian optimism: "There is more day to dawn. The sun is but a morning star."

Perhaps for many it was his greatest contribution that he was true to his principles and practiced his ideals, that he showed others by his example how to live "a special kind of life, not just think about

*The end of man, or that which is prescribed by
the eternal or immutable dictates of reason, and not
suggested by vague and transient desires, is the
highest and most harmonious development of his
powers to a complete and consistent whole.*

Wilhelm von Humboldt, quoted by J. S. Mill in *On Liberty,*
Chapter III.

---

one." What Krutch suggested over two decades ago is dramatically
clear today: Thoreau has truly become a "prophetic figure." The
new age could not do better than to "honor his metaphysics as well
as his humanity."

Akin in spirit to Condorcet, Jefferson, Emerson, and Thoreau is
the thought of John Stuart Mill. Nobody has spoken on the subject
of individuality more eloquently than he did in the essay *On
Liberty*. Acknowledging the inspiration of the liberal-minded Ger-
man philosopher, Wilhelm von Humboldt, Mill condemned the pressures exerted on the individual both by conventional society and by
governments. That way, he said, lie conformity, mediocrity and
inertia. Society will truly progress, he maintained, when its individual members are liberated from coercion, both legal and social.
Improvement, which he was careful to distinguish from mere change,
can come about only through originality whose source is to be
found nowhere but in the genius of the individual.

"It will not be denied by anybody that originality is
a valuable element in human affairs. There is always need of persons not only to discover new truths . . . but also to commence new
practices. . . . Genius can only breathe freely in an *atmosphere* of
freedom. . . . The initiation of all wise or noble things comes and
must come from individuals; generally at first from some one individual."[147]

Such was Mill's faith in the virtue of individuality freely expressed
that there were none whom he excluded from equal consideration.
"There ought to be no pariahs," he proclaimed, "in a full-grown and
civilised nation; no persons disqualified, except through their own
default."[148] From no source should the springs of talent be denied

the opportunity to flow. In particular Mill, who owed so much to the inspiration of his wife, was an eloquent advocate of feminine emancipation, one of his major works being *The Subjection of Women.*

With these changes of emphasis, the belief in the priority of the individual ran its varied course from the 16th through the 19th centuries. If the earlier stress, as in Machiavelli, was laid on *virtu* (with its connotations of masculinity, force, and skill), later thinkers from Condorcet to Mill exalted reason and virtue in its ethical sense. The individuality which they conceived was compatible with consideration for others. They lauded the individual will, but fortified it with conscience.

Since the second half of the 19th century, however, business and industry, science and technology, war and revolution, have produced a mounting accumulation of effects upon society. These in their turn have set in motion new crosscurrents of opinion, some diametrically opposite to one another.

At one pole are those who carry the notion of individuality to its ultimate stage of justice. Examples of this in action are the ideal entrepreneur competing to outwit and destroy a business rival, or the governments of nation-states exercising at home and abroad what they call their sovereignty—the unlimited right to do as they wish.

Similarly in the psychology of individual development, we can also observe the effects of this doctrine in its extreme form. If individualized teaching is carried too far, children may be asked to learn (and, occasionally, to create) in isolation and not be given an opportunity to work cooperatively in a group. As Martin Buber says, the individual as a creator is a lonely figure; expression which is merely individual and has no reference to others can be a matter of "beating [one's] wings in a void."[149] This kind of psychological isolation is fostered by the patterns of life in the larger society. Particularly in the cities, there is seldom a neighborhood for the very simple reason that people do not know their neighbors. What Riesman calls "the lonely crowd" then becomes a reality, so that individuals experience alienation and anomie.

At the other pole, people have responded to such practices and attitudes by a reversal of priorities. They have pitted collectivism against individualism, socialism or communism against capitalism or liberalism. Marx and Engels were vigorous in denouncing the existing system, but vague about the ideal which was to follow its violent overthrow. They did not offer a conception of how people could live together cooperatively and in an equalitarian community. Extreme collectivists have emphasized the duties of individuals, but neglected their rights; they have acquiesced in social restraints and governmental coercion at the expense of personal freedom. When pushed too far, the result can be an all-controlling super-organization. Big Brother in 1984 was not pure fiction. Hitler and Stalin are among the stark realities of this century.

The isolated beings whom we mentioned as the product of an excessive individualism can easily become the victims of the totalitarian controller. Because they are already divided, his conquest is easy. He demands that they obey some larger force, some mythical higher interest—"the will of the people," "the national interest," "the public safety," "the Aryan race," "the dictatorship of the proletariat," "the divinity of the Emperor." Even Rousseau allowed himself to write: "When the prince says to [the citizen] : 'It is expedient for the State that you should die,' he ought to die...."[150] Thus, the secretary-general of the British Communist Party could tell a young poet in the nineteen-thirties that it was his duty to fight and be killed in the Spanish Civil War because the party needed a literary martyr.

But the point that any doctrine can be perverted when pushed to excess should not blind us to the truth that in moderate form it can be valuable. Just as Condorcet, Jefferson, Emerson, Thoreau, and Mill were able to supply a beneficent concept of individuality, so can the claims of society—our duties to others and our membership in broader communities—be interpreted consistently with human good. It is to this topic that we now turn.

The quest for a universal society

If it was fashionable a century ago to glorify the virtues of the self, and to envisage one's relations with others as a competition in self-assertiveness, much of the philosophy of the 20th century has laid stress on human sociability and our need for cooperation with others of our kind. Hence in the 20th century various social philosophies have focused on what the group contributes to the individual and how the latter reciprocally serves the group, rather than concentrating on what each can accomplish and acquire individually. Concepts of this kind have brought into prominence other values than those stressed by the individualists. Love, altruism, benevolence, self-sacrifice, service to others, modesty, humility, tolerance, humanitarianism—these have been more extolled (i.e. ranked higher on the hierarchies of these social philosophers) than selfishness, power, aggressiveness, and their customary accompaniments. In fact, the evidence multiplies around us that a values revolution is already under way and that its ideals are being voiced by many of today's youth and by humanitarian adults.

One aspect of this revolution of which none can fail to be aware is a crisis of authority. All established authorities the world over are nowadays being questioned and challenged. This is as true of presidents, prime ministers and popes as it is of university and business executives. Institutions which seemed solid and secure a couple of decades ago are shaking at their foundations. For when the basic values of a society are being reexamined, its component organizations will necessarily be replanned and restructured.

In the social order prevailing in the middle decades of this century, the central pillar of the structure has been the nation-state. But today, both its ethics and its efficiency are under attack. Many consider it obsolescent; some think it already obsolete. For there are two basic social needs of humanity which the traditional nation-state not only cannot satisfy, but actually prevents. One is the universal need of the entire human race to recognize its oneness and organize this planet for future survival and well-being. The other need, equally pressing, is to rediscover and recreate the small community, the intimate grouping of neighbors who live together in daily association and can help one another and benefit through mutual aid. The nation-state is an outmoded structure because it is too large for some fundamental purposes and too small for others. The Good Society, which the Good Person seeks, will come about through a combination of world order and small community. And already there are signs that these changes are under way.

It is highly significant that contemporary world organizations—those which transcend the nation-state—are themselves raising their sights above and beyond the narrow limits of conventional horizons. In this, they are continuing a long and honorable tradition. There were famous occasions in the past when higher values, which marked a notable improvement on the ethics then prevailing, were explicitly drafted and ratified by official agencies or groups of citizens serving in a public capacity. Together these have constituted some of the milestones in our uneven ascent to higher levels of civilization. In the Western World Magna Carta, the Petition of Right, the Declaration of the Rights of Man and the Citizen furnish examples, interweaving, as they do, the political history of England, the United States, and France, across a span of seven and a half centuries. Since each later document was founded on, and incorporated, the experience of those which preceded, the most recent and the ambitious attempt in this lengthening series should be considered here. This one happens to be of special relevance in a study of values, since all the previous formulations of the higher values of the human race attained their culmination and synthesis in the Universal Declaration of Human Rights—adopted by the General Assembly of the United Nations in December 1948 without a negative vote.[151]

In the long history of such declarations (whether by the world's religions, by moral philosophers, or by public bodies) this document has a place which is unique and a significance thus far without parallel. It was painstakingly elaborated after a thorough study and comparison of all similar efforts conducted earlier. It was carefully discussed and debated, clause by clause and word by word, in meetings which extended over nearly two years. It set out to be both comprehensive in content and universal in scope. Finally, it was adopted officially as a statement of principles, applying to all human beings, by the international body with the widest membership which mankind has achieved to date.

These aspects of the Declaration were stressed both at the time of its adoption and in subsequent evaluations of its importance. The Preamble itself reads as follows: "The General Assembly proclaims this Universal Declaration of Human Rights as *a common standard of achievement for all peoples and all nations,* to the end that every individual and every organ of society, keeping this Declaration constantly in mind, shall strive by teaching and education to promote respect for these rights and freedoms and by progressive measures, national and international, to secure their universal and effective recognition and observance, both among the peoples of Member States themselves and among the peoples of territories under their jurisdiction."[152] The thirty articles of the text which follows this preamble have been described "as an international Magna Carta or an international charter of human rights."[153] As such, it should be emphasized, the Declaration is not an international treaty, nor is it legally binding on the governments of member-states. It does, however, possess the highest moral authority—both because it "is certainly the most comprehensive, the first Declaration in history to set forth the rights and freedoms to which men and women everywhere are entitled"[154] and because it expresses officially the position of the United Nations. For these reasons, in the course of the last twenty years, it has been widely cited in judicial decisions of national courts, in the texts of international agreements and the discussions of international conferences, and its influence is equally discernible in recent constitutions and legislation.

To mark the twentieth anniversary of its adoption of the Declaration, the United Nations conducted an International Conference on Human Rights, attended by representatives of eighty-four states, in Teheran during April and May 1968. This was "the first conference ever organized on a world-wide basis to consider the question of human rights in all its aspects."[155] The Conference unanimously adopted a proclamation which affirmed: "The Universal Declaration of Human Rights states a common understanding of the peoples of the world concerning the inalienable and inviolable rights of all members of the human family and constitutes an obligation for the members of the international community."[156]

Intentionally, the content of the Universal Declaration was phrased so as to be all-embracing—its more specific, detailed application being left to the two Covenants which were drafted later and have yet to be adopted by member-governments. The thirty articles of the text may be grouped and summarized as follows:

1. Articles 1–5. These affirm the basic right of each person to be regarded as somebody equal, unique and independent—namely, the rights to life, liberty and personal security. Slavery and cruel forms of punishment are prohibited. Most importantly, the United Nations has proclaimed its image of human beings as creatures both intelligent and moral, an image applying equally to all humans without exception or distinction.

2. Articles 6–12 are concerned with a person's civil rights before the law. They assert the fundamental principles in the administration of justice to which laws, courts, and judges must conform. Equal protection is stressed; discrimination and arbitrariness are banned.

3. The next three Articles cover those political rights to which an individual is entitled in the relations between states—the rights of free movement across frontiers, of asylum, and of nationality.

4. In Articles 16–20, the Declaration sets out the fundamental freedoms pertaining to marriage, acquisition of property, the expression of opinion.

5. These are followed, in Article 21, by the insistence on political freedom, through government based on the will of the people.

6. The subsequent articles turn to another group of rights which give the Declaration its 20th-century flavor, as contrasted with the American and French Declarations of the 18th century. The Proclamation of Teheran (1968) has stated the point this way (in clause 13): "Since human rights and fundamental freedoms are indivisible, the full realization of civil and political rights without the enjoyment of economic, social and cultural rights, is impossible." Consequently, Articles 22–25 of the Universal Declaration embrace the basic rights of the individual within the economy and as a recipient of social security.

7. Then come two Articles, 26–27, whose subject is the right of all human beings to be educated and to have equal access to the cultural life of the community.

8. Finally, in Articles 28–30, the Declaration affirms not only the right of human beings to an international order in which all of these rights can be respected, but also their duties to their fellow-men generally.

Grandiose and comprehensive though this Declaration is, the human quest for civilization—our need ever to rise to higher ethical levels—will not end here. The United Nations Office of Public Information has well said of the thirty articles: "Every great act in history is a product of its age. The Declaration is no exception. It represents the spirit of the mid-20th century and embodies ideas and ideals of different races, cultures, beliefs or religions in the present age. As man marches forward, he will discover new horizons of larger freedom and new concepts of a fuller and better life." The ultimate apex of the hierarchy of values is a vision dimly seen, but always to be sought.

That the search continues may also be observed in the case of another institution, whose name, like the United Nations, signifies a universality which its membership has not yet attained: the Catholic Church.[157] In the course of its history, popes and councils as well as individual theologians (such as Thomas Aquinas) have repeatedly expounded their conceptions of a hierarchy of values. The latest of these is the most remarkable and, in some respects, the most original. It bears the stamp of a human being of rare greatness, Pope John XXIII, who initiated the modernizing (*aggiornamento*) of a tradition-ridden organization.

In two of the Encyclicals which marked his papacy, *Mater et Magistra* and *Pacem in Terris*, John XXIII formulated his version of the basic rights of mankind, versions which, as he acknowledged,[158] owe much to the United Nation's Universal Declaration. Continuity with Catholic tradition is expressed in these documents in the attention given to the family ("the natural, primary cell of human society"),[159] as in the affirmation that human rights are grounded in a natural law which derives from God. But to John XXIII, tradition was not a terminus, but a point of departure. More than any pope before him, he insisted on the rights of women, both within the family and outside, and on the right of each individual to be educated to the level of his or her abilities. More than his predecessors were willing to concede, Pope John extended the conception of natural rights to embrace the economic and social rights of individuals.

Further than that, this true social democrat—born of peasant stock and always at home with the common people—declared himself unequivocally for democracy as the system of government which has the most respect for the freedom and dignity of the individual. So consistently did John XXIII accept democracy that he also applied it to the freedom of religion—of any religion, that is—something which would have sounded like heresy to most of his predecessors.

The same liberalism permeated his international outlook. Since peace was the highest ideal for the family of nations to pursue, this pope quietly dropped the old hue and cry for "holy wars." His preference was to coexist and cooperate with other systems (despite the "errors" of their philosophies) when in practice they were following the paths of peace. Human rights, moreover, were not those of the privileged elite or of a few favored nations or peoples. There was no room in Pope John's humanity for doctrines of a master-race or an imperial mission. All peoples everywhere have an equal right to their independence. Rights, in short, are the common stock of the human race. They are universal in range and their content is the same for all.

The virtue of the small community

Necessary though it is to create frameworks for a world order, since without them survival is problematic, these by themselves can not make the good society. For this must begin with small groups of people who seek better ways to live by working together in intimate face-to-face relationships. From taking part in mutually enhancing activities, each individual will grow in a highly personal way. The key concepts for such groupings have always been participation, cooperation, and community. Although numerous cooperatives have developed for purely economic purposes, the small communities which will best contribute to individual growth and to a world society are those which help people to find superior life styles and to act in common for common ends. In this way, they can learn to master the art of living.

Why is it that we need small communities for this to happen? The answer lies in our predispositions and preferences. Fundamentally, we are social creatures who need the company of our kind in order to be human. It is in integrated groups of limited size that we live best and, fortunately, we prefer living in this fashion. Since this is the case, and since we cannot learn or grow psychologically as individuals except in company with our fellows, both our survival and the development of our humanness make it essential that we re-create the small community. It is in such an intimate communal group that we discover how to live through participating and experiencing, the only way which is humanly meaningful.

The concept of the psychic unity of mankind, however, inspiring, will remain an abstraction which cannot be truly understood until each person has felt it vividly in a situation of trust and mutual reciprocity. Obviously it is impossible to see, hear, talk with, and relate to, all of our fellow human beings directly and immediately. For this kind of communication, the group has to be of manageable proportions. A good community may consist of a dozen families or even less. The optimum size cannot be determined, and will doubtless vary with place and time. But we do know that such groups should be small enough to allow face-to-face contacts to occur regularly. Also, they must have a sense of psychological privacy.

In contrast to the large aggregates (a metropolis, for example) where loneliness increases with size and distance, small groups can be a never-ending experience in sociability. Not only do they profoundly influence the individual's life, but quite literally they are a way of life. Far from being homogenous and stereotyped, such groups have been of many kinds. Some have evolved more or less organically; others have been intentional. The former include the primary groups based on kinship (the tribe or clan), those that belong together because of geography (a neighborhood group such as the Danish Folk High Schools established by Grundtvig or Jane Addams' Hull House), and certain long-established religious communities which have maintained unbroken traditions of democratic group life from prefeudal times (the Dukhobors, Hutterites, Mennonites, Waldensians).[160] The second kind—the intentional community—often involves the decision to form a new group for idealistic or practical purposes (e.g. the Mayflower Compact, Oneida in New York, Brook Farm in Massachusetts, New Harmony in Indiana, the Israeli kibbutzim), or for education (such schools as Summerhill or those that are educational and artistically productive as well, like the Bauhaus Centers).

The essence of the small community is that its activities are cooperative, its relations reciprocal. All participate in a joint effort in which all benefit. The result is something to which each contributes and which none can carry forward as effectively alone. Those groups which truly become communities (and are more than mere aggregations or neighborhoods) extend to their members equality of consideration and respect. Good will permeates a good community. This is the setting which affords a natural training-school (the Greek *paideusis*) for democracy in its original sense of active participation. It not only supplies the needed models, but also serves as both testing ground and stage. Here is where people can become active, informed, and responsible citizens when they understand that the system is sensitive to their participation. Here is where personal growth occurs through cooperation and in service freely given for the good of others. The feelings which can make this possible range from friendship through trust and sympathy to love. In the groups which these sentiments inspire, each of us can become vividly aware that we have friends, as well as workmates and playmates, and that all of these help us find a social identity and become better versions of ourselves.

But how, it may be asked, can small communities be created? "Every person" says Arthur E. Morgan in *The Small Community*, "can learn the fundamentals of community life by learning to live in harmony and good will with the person next to him."[161] Each of us, in other words, can first begin acquiring the art of community in our daily relationships. These are the natural building-blocks for the eventual structure which can house the family of humanity. And they lie everywhere around us in immediate reach. People cannot

*You can hardly pick up a newspaper or turn on
your TV these days without coming up against some
melancholy character complaining about the
helplessness of the individual. The ordinary decent
American, according to the current clichés, is
numbered, computerized, victimized, and deper-
sonalized by a lot of big institutions and monstrous
forces beyond his understanding or control.*

*Well, it's all too true, and you can get plenty of
testimony from the young men caught in the draft,
the old pensioners caught in the inflation, the workers
laid off by the recession, and the millions who can't
even afford to get sick. Even the railroads and the
steel companies, and the President of the United States
himself, are muttering about being trapped by things
beyond their influence.*

*And yet, if you look around, it is hard to avoid a
paradox in all this. For here and there the people are
stirring, and organizing to regain their sovereignty.
Not since the days of the New Deal in America
has there been so much insistent questioning of the
institutions and purposes of America as there is now,
and not without evidence of progress either.*

*These are not mass movements as yet. In fact, they
are comparatively small. But slowly, citizens' groups
are forming to protect the environment of their
communities, to challenge the assumptions and
priorities of their elected officials, to defend the
average consumer from the commercial gougers, and
to work in many other ways for the improvement
of American life.*

James Reston, "The Quiet Revolution," *International Herald
Tribune*, January 16–17, 1971.

---

*The beginning point for community development
is person-to-person relationships. . . . Almost every
problem of the community, state, and nation, is
met with on a small scale in our relations with people
closest to us. This is not a rhetorical expression,
but a statement of specific fact. Unless we can be
successful in those relationships we have not yet
mastered the art of building a community. We do not
need to wait for great programs. Each person in
his day-to-day relationships . . . can be mastering the
art of community.*

*Regardless of the forms of government and of society,
most of our contacts from week to week and from
year to year are these first-hand personal relations
with people close to us. If these relations are fine, then
the greater part of our lives is fine, and that fineness
will constantly infect the community and all social
units beyond the community.*

Arthur E. Morgan, *The Small Community*, New York:
Harper and Bros., 1942, pp. 116–17.

---

bring peace to the world who cannot bring harmony to a neighborhood.

Examples occur everywhere of the kind of project which a small community can develop by spontaneous mutual aid. Information about them, however, is seldom well publicized. This became abundantly clear in the preparation of an anthology for high school students which focused, among other things, on improvements in human relations and on social activities of an altruistic nature. It was difficult to find articles illustrating how ordinary people cooperate and extend themselves for others. Most of what is available on such topics is printed in those magazines or sections of newspapers which are designed for women readers.

In Reedsport, a small town on the Oregon coast, there is a one-armed former logger, now a dog-catcher, who has worked for several years on his own initiative to create a garden city. Empty blocks and unused corners have been beautified with flowers, trees, and bushes. Small areas of potential beauty which were not valued by their owners were cleared of rubbish, weeds and brambles. With sensitive imagination, this man succeeded in making friends with many of the people whose dogs were destructive to plants. Not only did the latter then control their dogs, but they made gifts to the dog-catcher of plants to be placed at some corner or curbside. Such a concern for natural beauty within an urban environment is as important as an art gallery or museum. It may even be more salutary to human well-being.

In 1970, a young Danish couple moved into a small residential community north of Copenhagen. The wife, a university graduate in psychology, had a long interest in cooperatives, consumer buying, graphic arts, and crafts. Within a few months, many of the house-wives were combining their talents. One who was an expert seam-stress helped others with sewing. A girl from a seacoast town taught all who wanted to learn how to knit mittens of untreated wool simi-lar to those worn by Icelandic fishermen. Others shared their skills in cooking and woodworking. Childcare was also a mutual enter-prise. The block became an extended family and all the children were welcomed in all homes much in the manner of the Mutual Adoption Club (M.A.C.) in Aldous Huxley's *Island.* The fathers also shared in the neighborhood activities, and families with cars took turns as responsible agents for neighborhood shopping.

For those who care to look for them examples abound of con-structive community service by socially-minded individuals and of new patterns of association in small groups. The latter may be less stable than those of the past because of the mobility of a modern population. But if they are to serve the function of a true community, they will continue, as of old, to be based on mutual helpfulness. Few clusters of people are more transitory than college students. Yet for many individuals, their college years are the one time in their lives when they feel some sense of belonging to an integrated community.

At the same time, before leaving this subject, we would do well to remind ourselves that all ideals can be corrupted and that no human society—not even the small community—is free from danger or im-perfections. There are some independent spirits for whom the very smallness may become stifling. Being small, a community may be fearful of deviations; it may insist on conformity to a single pattern. The intentional community runs the further risk of being too meticu-lously planned. If directed from on high, its members will lose the

*Every MAC (Mutual Adoption Club) consists of
anything from fifteen to twenty-five assorted
couples. Newly elected brides and bridegrooms, old
timers with growing children, grandparents and
great-grandparents—everybody in the club adopts
everyone else. . . . Making twenty families grow
where only one grew before. This is an inclusive,
unpredestined, voluntary family. Twenty pairs
of fathers and mothers, eight or nine ex-fathers and
ex-mothers, and forty or fifty assorted children of
all ages. . . . [The result:] Healthier relationships
in more responsible groups, wider sympathies and
deeper understandings. . . . Mutual adoption
guarantees children against injustice and the worst
consequences of parental ineptitude. [But] it increases
the number of their responsibilities; it exposes them
to a wide variety of disciplines. . . . If a child
feels unhappy in his first home, we do our best for
him in fifteen or twenty second homes. Meanwhile the
father and mother get some tactful therapy from the
other members of their Mutual Adoption Club.
But . . . it is not only when they are in trouble that
children resort to their deputy parents and grandparents. They do it all the time, whenever they
feel the need for a change or some kind of new
experience. And it isn't just a social whirl . . . [There
are] Duties as well as privileges in a big, open,
unpredestined, inclusive family. . . .*

Aldous Huxley, *Island*, London: Chatto and Windus, 1962,
pp. 90–93.

---

vital sense of creative participation. Small communities are not
immune from the tyranny of a single autocrat. Moreover, if the
group is preoccupied with looking inward, it will become self-
centered and then static. Small groups can breed small minds if they

wield an exclusive domination over one's interests and activities. Gossip, malice, and spite can be deadly when directed at close range. Smallness is no protection against low standards, banality, and parochialism.

For the person to grow in a healthy manner, the group must look outward as well as inward. That is why the microcosm needs the macrocosm, just as surely as the converse. As D. H. Lawrence has written: "The cure would consist in bringing about a state of honesty and a certain trust among a group of people, or many people—if possible, all the people in the world."[162] The union of the Lilliputian and the universal, their synergy in fact, will be the operative secret of the good society, the seed-bed of the good person.

Self-actualizing individuals and mass progress

Can we say that mankind at large is moving any closer to the values we have just discussed? Are there signs that we are changing in ways that would indicate a higher level of humanness? Are we succeeding in finding more community with others as well as expanding our inner capacities? Humanity makes progress, as we understand the term, when two things happen. When people in general consciously aim at higher values than previously, and when increasing numbers come closer in practice to actualizing them. The loftiness of the ideal and the spread of the real are equally important; both are necessary if true progress is to occur.

When we observe our contemporary world, the evidence is contradictory. On the one hand, it could be plausibly argued that the 20th century thus far is the most violent in history. Look at the front page of the morning paper and see what it is filled with most days of the week. Governments continue to engage in what Aldous Huxley has called "the organized lovelessness of war"[163]—sometimes against their own peoples. The combined current expenditures of the "developed" nations for this purpose amount to thirty times more than what they allot for aid to underdeveloped countries. Crime rates apparently rise along with affluence—some even say because of it. Human survival is imperilled by a growing number of adverse conditions: the dangerous rate of population growth, the risk of annihilation by nuclear bombs, the burden of armaments in general, an industrial technology which seems to be completely out of hand, the systematic pollution of land, air, and water, the gap between the "haves" and the "have nots," are continuing discrimination between the sexes, races and religions.

Strangely enough, all this is taking place along with signs of improvement which give us valid grounds for hope. It is the paradox of this century that all its senseless destruction, cruel injustice and criminal wastefulness are accompanied by a notable increase in acts of humanitarianism and compassion. This is the century, after all, which launched the first two serious attempts at the beginnings of world organization, which has recorded genuine gains in the direction of democracy and, therefore, of greater respect for human dignity, which has seen more and more governments provide help on a national basis for their citizens who are handicapped, poor, or unfortunate. Increasingly, people are protesting against conditions in which they once aquiesced. The conviction has dawned that, if human beings are capable of reaching the moon, we can cure the ills of our planet.

Along with these developments in public policy, significant changes have occurred in the attitudes and feelings, what could best be called the conscience, of ordinary men and women. In fact, a number of 20th century thinkers are saying that we are becoming more human and that the future will be better than the past. Robert S. Morison, a philosopher-scientist, believes that the changes we see all about us are largely for the good: "The over-all course of human development and culture has been upward in most measurable senses."[164] If we ask more specifically how this is happening, we see several trends all of which point to the growth of human character and, what Sorokin has called altruistic love. Catherine Roberts, after a careful study of the "educated" conscience, concludes that there is a growing unwillingness to inflict suffering. Martin Buber spent a lifetime studying the "I-Thou" relationship in which one becomes aware that "all real living is meeting."[165] He discerns a gradual restructuring of society toward decentralization which, he thinks, underlies all economic and social evolution. This tendency is allied, in his judgment, with "something that is slowly evolving in the human soul: the most intimate of resistances—resistance to mass or collective loneliness."[166]

Others, while being unsparing in their social criticism, see what is happening in even more positive terms. Mumford has this to say:

"In man, the blind forces that· stirred through matter and organic life have now achieved, as never before, a consciousness that reaches ever further back into origins and ever further forward into possible choices and possible destinies. Despite many setbacks and diversions, mind has matured, and love, which first sprang out of the needs of reproduction and nurture, has widened its domain. No theory of human development is adequate that does not include this widening of the province of love. . . ."[167]

And Reich announces with a sense of inevitability the coming of a change of consciousness, a movement to a higher level of values.

"There is a revolution coming. It will not be like revolutions of the past. It will originate with the individual and with culture, and it will change the political structure only as its final act. . . . It is now spreading with amazing rapidity. . . . It promises a higher reason, a more human community, and a new and liberated individual. . . . This is the revolution of the new generation."[168]

As we have seen, the evolution toward the good person and the good society is already occurring, and can be furthered by simultaneous improvements in several directions. We need, not only the universal acceptance of the United Nations Declaration of Rights and the principles of Pope John XXIII, but also the speeding up of the decentralization movements to which Buber referred, the re-creating of the small community.

Beyond these, there is a further important influence that must not be overlooked—the contributions of people with exceptional gifts. Bertrand Russell, for instance, has suggested that the world has been significantly shaped by the contributions of one hundred outstanding individuals. On a retrospective view of the past, as well as a survey of the present, these seem to fall into two major groups which are polar opposites: the social leaders and the creative intellectuals. The influence of the former, when judged in terms of positive human evolution, is often negative and sometimes downright evil. Their use of power has frequently had the effect of depriving people of their freedom and in all too many cases of their lives. Their level of character growth (see "The stages of individual development," Chapter Four) is generally low. Some are merely expedient and opportunistic; others are frankly immoral. Whether they are operating in government, in business, in a trade union, or in a university, their techniques are those of power plays and conspiracy. Powermongers, in the style described by Machiavelli, have often acted as if lies and deceit were the essence of statecraft. Theirs is an unbroken tradition extending from Plato's "Phoenician Lie" to our contemporary "Credibility Gap." As between the alternative priorities of society or the individual, what they prefer is autonomy for themselves and conformity for others.

Opposed to the social leaders throughout history have been the creative intellectuals. The qualities which these value include spontaneity, uniqueness, personal growth, imagination, originality, experiments with the unconventional and the untried. In J. B. Priestley's terms, they belong to the loose world and the social leaders to the tight. More than any others in society, it is the creative intellectuals who generate and develop the ideas from which our values spring. But the creative intellectuals themselves show two tendencies. All too many of them, including some of the greatest geniuses, remain or become egotists and psychological cripples. They find it hard enough to live socially with others, let alone to reach out in a spirit of altruistic love. There are others, however, who become self-actualizing and who, like Jane Addams and Martin Luther King, devote themselves to humanity. In terms of the discussion earlier in this chapter, it is surely significant, that the unsociable geniuses who serve their own egos are able to emerge under conditions of excessive individualism—in the Italian Renaissance, for example, or in the concrete jungles of our large modern cities. But humanitarian altruists, who seek to serve to needs of others, flourish best in the atmosphere of a good family in a good community.

Since it is persons of this kind who can best help humanity to emerge on to a higher plane, we should inquire whether their numbers and influence may be growing. Among adults who are now in their so-called "prime of life," a few active spirits are suggesting positive programs. But for their values to take effect, there must be tens of thousands of creative innovators and catalysts as well as a mass acceptance of their ideas. Fortunately, the evidence multiplies that the number of gifted youth is on the increase, that these are also undergoing a change of consciousness, and that what they emphasize is the growth of the person and the community. Platt has argued persuasively that an explosion of genius is occuring among today's youth.[169] In like vein, the physicist Dennis Gabor believes that we may be entering an era when the general level of intelligence will rise far above the present, both in quality and quantity.[170]

If parallel improvements take place on the ethical plane, one may anticipate the future of humanity with hope. Already, there are encouraging signs which point in this direction. Both among the young and the not-so-young, we can see today more concern for the unfortunate, more revulsion against war, more determination to take positive steps to remove injustices. In more and more homes, the children are invited into the family councils and their opinions are sought. Perhaps that is why, as they mature, they are unwilling to acquiesce in the authoritarian structures of the big systems they encounter— whether governmental, corporate, or educational. Service in the civil rights movement or the Peace Corps, so prevalent in the early nineteen sixties, has been followed by protests against war, research and action on behalf of the consumers, and a crusade against the industrial destroyers of nature. In the various communes, collectives, and cooperatives, many of the members are seeking to live by the ethics of altruism. Numerous recent graduates in professions which were once so conservative are preferring to work for the poor and for other minorities than for those who are already rich and powerful. The movement for women's liberation is infusing into the lifestream of society the feminine values which are closer to those of Jesus than of Juggernaut. The "Golden Day" has not yet dawned; but the dark night may be starting to pale.

In addition to the rise of our values to higher levels, what is truly significant nowadays is their extension to ever-widening circles of participants. Gone, or fast going, are the oligarchical limitations by which most of the earlier hierarchies of values were restricted. In the modern world, many of the decisive tendencies contribute to democratization. The major religions, the pathbreaking inventions, the more humane ethics, the most useful institutions, ideas of justice —these become, or can become, the common heritage of all mankind. A word that is spoken, a thought once expressed, a technique revealed, ceases to belong to its author. No one has a copyright over

*The further electoral rights are extended, the
greater is the need for extending them; for after each
concession the strength of the democracy increases,
and its demands increase with its strength. . . .
The exception at last becomes the rule, concession
follows concession, and no stop can be made short of
universal suffrage.*

Alexis de Tocqueville, Democracy in America.

---

beneficent change. This can develop and grow without any other limits than those of its own demonstrated goodness and relevance. Humanity at large is, or can be, the beneficiary of all the good which individuals create—or equally the victim of all the evil.

The dynamics of this relation between the socially creative and concerned and the mass of mankind suggest how the good person and the good society may eventually evolve together. Theirs is not a circular relationship. It is possible, but difficult, for an individual to become the self-actualizing good person without the environmental support and influences of the good society. In contrast, the good society, whether on the small scale or universally, cannot emerge unless it be composed of, or led by, a sufficiency of good persons. What these are depends on the capacity to actualize the highest values. It is, therefore, to a discussion of these that we finally turn.

CHAPTER SEVEN

The higher values and the higher synthesis

Plato had a profound insight when he applied to the individual the same concepts of goodness or evil as he did to society and when he traced within the microcosm the identical virtues or vices which the macrocosm possessed. Here we have similarly had in mind an ideal of the good which applies equally to one or many, to the private realm or the public, to solitude or society. Such an ideal is relevant to the three images of mankind which see us as a mixture of good and evil, as basically good, or as capable of transcendence; but not to those which consider us bad animals or as malleable by any influence, however pernicious.

In general, people choose what they value and value what they choose. This does not prevent them, however, from making choices that are perverse or later regretting a choice they have made. By their choices people give meaning to their lives. To the extent that we are self-aware, we do this deliberately; at other times we are unaware of the act of choosing. Some deny that they make choices at all, claiming that they are victimized by acts of God or whims of Fate.

> As flies to wanton boys, are we to the gods,
> They kill us for their sport.[171]

As is axiomatic, the highest good is composed of the highest values, which cluster at the top of the hierarchy. These are the values which have been reaffirmed by every major philosophy and religion and are basic to what is known as the "perennial philosophy."[172] But they have often been ignored and neglected in the 20th century and sometimes disavowed. They form the triad: truth, beauty and love. These correspond to three basic aspects of human nature through which we relate ourselves to our environment and communicate with our fellowmen. Truth is the cognitive aspect; beauty, the aesthetic; love, the affective. Functioning as a unity, these three values present a vision of wholeness to human beings and provide what is essential to our humanness. Since these ideals constitute the highest good, they signify the deepest potentialities which each of us seeks to realize.

One of the biases of the modern world, however, is that it has overemphasized the cognitive and ascribed to reason a virtual monopoly of knowledge. Correspondingly, it has neglected the aesthetic and the affective and, along with them, their related values of beauty and love. Not only has the spiritual realm been ruled out of bounds, but faith is no longer deemed a valid way of obtaining insight. Yet there is a fundamental truth in the statements of John XXIII that "human society is primarily a spiritual reality," and "a society that is welded together by force is not human."[173] Moreover, when Keats reminded us that "Beauty is truth, truth beauty," he was extolling truth for its beauty and not the reverse. So, too, Schiller contended that "until man, in his physical and sensuous modes of being, has been accustomed to the laws of beauty, he is not capable of perceiving what is good and true—he is not capable of spiritual liberty."[174]

It is particularly in our educational system that we find the distortion of values and the resulting despair which many attribute to the priorities prevailing in society at large. Charles Silberman is one of an increasing number of writers who describe the American School as a "grim, joyless place" where children are "oppressed by petty, meaningless rules and the atmosphere is intellectually and aesthetically barren."[175] In other words, even the cognitive realm, as the schools generally interpret it, fails to satisfy the more inquiring minds. Most classroom teaching stays at the lower level, that of imparting facts and information.[176] Rarely is critical thinking stimulated or evaluation encouraged. Actual education, therefore, is far removed from what ideally it should be. "Education," Silberman con-

*Our stake is more than one in the survival of the
species. We want a species to survive that we can be
proud of. The chances are that life, some life,
would continue and evolve again into new and
different species, but none would be man. . . .
The future I want for my species is a society of
individuals each of whom plays a significant and in
some measure unique role in that society. It is a
society in which every man—as far as it is humanly
possible—is free from outer and inner restrictions
which would prevent the richest development of his
unique combination of capacities. It is a society,
not without tensions, but one in which no man need
fear his neighbor, and no man need fear himself.
It is a world society which welcomes any number
of cultural subdivisions, and counts them all of value.*

*No such society now exists, and none can exist
unless the majority of the members of it are possessors
of a kind of character structure which is not now
common. What is needed then is a radical transfor-
mation of personalities, not in terms of modes of
adjustment, but in terms of moral character.*

Anne Roe, "The Behavioral Sciences," in Robert Ulich, ed.,
Education and Mankind, New York: Harcourt, Brace,
Jovanovich, Inc., 1964, p. 212–13.

---

tinues, "should prepare people not just to earn a living, but to live a
life, a creative, sensitive life. This means that the schools must provide a liberal, humanizing education."

The priorities of our society do not include beauty (particularly
that of nature) as necessary daily fare for the growing child,
although it was Wordsworth's opinion that the best education comes
through experiencing the beauty of nature and the natural human
feelings. Nourishment for the soul is thought to be of less moment
than keeping order and checking on attendance. If bodies are present, souls can fend for themselves. When schools are designed, there

is little recognition that art and nature have charms, like music, to soothe the savage breast. Similarly in the community at large, production costs and economic growth take precedence over such amenities as parks and shorelines, the preservation of wilderness and of vista points. The results of basing decisions on a rationale of cost accounting and the metric of efficiency confront us every day. Are they not very different from those which would provide aesthetic and affective fulfillment and lead to true knowledge, which is the understanding of the self?

The affective realm has at heart that human relationship which Buber termed communion. Such a relationship enables one person to know another. For this bond to be created, cooperation is vital. Yet the latter is rarely praised, except within an organization or team which is designed to fight against some other team or organization—as Plato noted that a band of robbers is united by its own code of justice to which its members must adhere. Love is never seriously proposed in public (except on Sundays) as a principle of harmonious social cohesion. Only those who seek community or who approach saintliness—such as the late Martin Luther King—advocate it as a life-style. When they attract followers, such apostles of love are thought to be dangerous. So much so, that they have often been destroyed by violence. Gandhi and King are two examples in this century. In contrast, competition, aggressiveness and war (the last of these euphemistically called "defense") are propagated with almost a religious zeal by the power elite and the strident majority. Many academics, as we have seen, study these phenomena assiduously (and often uncritically), while others apply their educated minds to the design and manufacture of the tools of violence which the powermen employ.

As a number of contemporary observers see it,[177] along its course our civilization swerved off the track, detouring onto a perilous side-journey with science and individualism in the engineer's cab. What has resulted is a values vacuum which accompanies our material affluence. This, in turn, has produced a growing cynicism among many of our elite, an increasing alienation of ever larger numbers of our intellectuals and our youth, and the bewilderment of people in general. As the highest values continue to be distorted and denied, it becomes daily more apparent that only by reaffirming them can humanity survive and be ennobled and the individual find both identity and community.

Although truth, beauty and love correspond to different sides of human nature, this does not mean that the cognitive, aesthetic and affective can exist in psychological isolation. To distinguish them helps the understanding; but in life, they are not separable. Our actual behavior derives from a "cognitive-emotional-motivational matrix," as one psychologist has phrased it, where no true separation is possible.[178] Each facet of the self serves as a way of linking the individual with others. It is through the unity of truth, beauty and love, that we express our relationship to the world. As ideals, these are, of course, abstractions and ultimates. Hence, they cannot be sharply defined or ever fully attained. But since the human creature, this "poor, bare forked animal"[179] that Shakespeare called us, is also an imaginative animal, the universal higher values bind all men together. By understanding truth, appreciating beauty, feeling love, we communicate with others. And does not communication create community?

As human beings, we are able to live together in society because, despite our uniqueness as individuals, fundamental similarities unite us all across the reach of space and time. When actualizing the highest values, we are therefore expressing both our universality and our uniqueness—the principle of complementarity mentioned earlier. In the quest for truth, beauty and love, we discover that differences, instead of implying conflict, may need one another for mutual support and may thus be harmonized within a higher synthesis.

Truth

Truth has been traditionally regarded as one of mankind's highest values. *Magna est veritas et praevalebit:* Truth is great and shall prevail. "Ye shall know the truth and it shall set you free." What is truth, however, has been variously conceived. If the road to hell is paved with good intentions, the route to heaven is marked with a medley of signs—all with a label of truth.

What does it mean to affirm that truth is one of the highest values to which we aspire? It means that the individual must first have knowledge in order to actualize his potentialities and live a good life. That knowledge must be accurate and reliable, and it should embrace as much as is humanly possible. It should extend outward to the cosmos and inward to the consciousness. "Know thyself" was the injunction of the Delphic Oracle; "learn about the universe" has been the common cry of physics and metaphysics.

Truth, however, is not simple, single, or undifferentiated. There is as much truth to be discovered as there is reality to be known. But not all aspects of reality have the same qualitative significance. It is true, for example, that various figures were printed in today's papers as yesterday's stockmarket prices. These are not as important, however, to the Good Person and the Good Society as the themes of the *Bible*, the *Republic*, *Hamlet*, or *War and Peace*. Some might say that the stockmarket is less important than a feature story on an ex-logger creating a garden city. On this general problem, Mumford comments:

> "We must be prepared to recognize that 'truths' do not stand together on a high and lofty pedestal: some are important and some are trivial, some are innocent and some are dangerous. . . . In a modern Western European community, a sociological insight into the causes and conditions of war and peace is a needed corrective . . . and without such correction, the mere increase of scientific knowledge, of which we boast so vacuously, may be highly inimical to the practice of the good life in the community."[180]

It is abundantly clear, as Polanyi has asserted, that some kinds of knowledge are superior to others.[181] Emerson, writing on love and friendship, expresses truth of a higher order than the annual balance sheet of General Motors. The Bill of Rights in the United States Constitution ranks as a greater truth than data about the "kill-ratio" in Vietnam. Where then shall we find the truth that will prevail and will set us free?

Of the many roads to truth, two are supported by a long tradition and have a special relevance today. One of these was first surveyed and sketched by Plato, was further mapped out by neo-Platonists, mystics, and transcendentalists, and is at present travelled by a growing number of humanistic scientists, philosophers, and artists— both young and old. Truth, on their view, is more than an attribute of the phenomena of perception, of this sensory world of fleeting, insubstantial shadows. They think that the reality of which we can have knowledge is infinite and, in the ultimate sense, a mystery. Truth is a feat of the imagination, and not simply a matter of verified experiment or linguistic analysis.

This formulation has more the touch of the artist than of the logician. Truth is to be divined rather than defined. It may well approximate Edith Sitwell's insight about poetry as "the flower of magic, not of logic."[182] The Platonists prefer synthesis over analysis, the infinite over the finite. Platonic truth does not seek exact boundaries, firm outlines, or exclusive categories. As Chagall said of the painting which he executed for the ceiling of the Paris Opera: "There is nothing precise in it. One cannot be precise and still be true." Each part belongs to a larger whole and everything flows into everything else.

An alternative path to truth—in fact, the main road since the Thomist *Summa*—began with Aristotle's syllogism, but has taken so many forks and meanderings that the modern terminus is a far distance from the point of origin. This route leads, via the Cartesian method and the English empiricists, to Newton's successors and so to experimental science and recent reductionism. In its physics as in its metaphysics, in logic as in language, this approach strives to be analytical. Every whole, on this reasoning, is a complex which you can only understand when you obtain a clear and distinct perception of its component parts. These divide into mutually exclusive categories. Reality is either this or it is that; what is A cannot also be not-A, and vice versa. Since anything which is present in the whole is assumed to reside somewhere in the parts, when the latter are reassembled knowledge of reality results.

A further development, which the originators of this method did not suggest, has commended itself to certain of their latter-day descendants. If the way to acquire knowledge is by subdividing the knowable, could one not treat the psychological the same as the logical and also subdivide the knower? Instead of the whole person thinking, each of us would don a set of masks, as it were, in order to play several roles when reasoning about this or that segment of the truth. Thus one arrives at those fictional characters—political man, economic man, scientific man, artistic man, and so on—whose performances were noted earlier.[183] The result is a series of truths in the plural—economic truth, scientific truth, artistic truth, etc. But the whole truth, as indivisible, is then reduced to a meaningless five-letter word.

The triumph of the scientific method, which established itself during the last three centuries as the royal way to truth, was the outcome of battles which scientists waged successfully in the 16th and 17th centuries against the Catholic Church. For a thousand years the Church had stood as the arbiter of truth in the Western World, and the whole weight of its authority was thrown behind any body of doctrine which it sanctioned—irrespective of whether the content was enlightened or specious or spurious. The strength of the Church was its faith: "Believe in the Lord Jesus Christ and ye shall be saved." But the religion which the Gospel of Jesus had inspired, and whose martyrs had resisted the power of Rome, suffered the fate of all spiritual revelations when they become institutionalized and powerful. It was a long descent from the Sermon on the Mount to the casuistries of canon law, from the transcendental love of Jesus touching the crippled child to sterile debates about how many angels could stand on the head of a pin, from the humility of the man from Nazareth to Roman claims of papal infallibility.

"During the Middle Ages" Paul Wienpahl has written, "a curious but powerful doctrine appeared—the doctrine of twofold truth. The two ways to truth are faith and reason. At first it was said that, if the two conflict, we must follow the lead of faith. . . ."[184] When the scientists, from Copernicus to Galileo to Newton, launched their series of discoveries and formulated new hypotheses in physics and astronomy, they did not initially seek to throw out religion but rather to prove it. Newton is said, for example, "to have written as much on theology as he wrote on 'natural philosophy.' "[185]

Out of this quest for new insights, however, developed what could only be called a new religion, for that is what science became for many. In its early stages this was conceived as serving a beneficent and moral purpose. The inventions which scientific discoveries ushered in might free mankind from the affliction of drudgery. Improved techniques of production could banish poverty by turning scarcities into abundance. Easier means of communication would widen the horizons of the mind, thereby enlarging the human community and liberating people from parochialism. Who could estimate the practical good that would be accomplished? Amid such hopes, Emerson himself was one of those who welcomed the new technology—that offshoot of scientific probing into the laws of the physical universe.

But the error of the scientists, as their work evolved, was that they, like the Church before them, went too far. In challenging the latter so that they could explore the truth, they not only discarded its theology, but more importantly, disregarded the spiritual needs which theology had recognized and the ethics which it upheld. For the "sacred cows" enshrined in the papal Bulls, the idolaters of science substituted their own golden calves, in particular the worship of the method. This mode of reasoning—hypothesis followed by experiment followed by verification or disproof—they professed to be objective and uninfluenced by personal preferences. The truth that would liberate was value-free.

Following this track and imbued with all the confidence of the Enlightenment, science was caught in the quicksands of its own reasoning. Scientific leaders in the 19th century and the mass of scientific workers in the 20th followed the route of objective research ever further from the older concepts of truth, until their doctrines, too, became as narrow and rigid a dogma as those of the Church had been. Reason, for them, attained its apotheosis in the perfecting of the scientific method. In this way, what had earlier been an assault on faith, as buttressed by religion, ended in the dedication to a new faith. Something of the zealotry and proselytizing fervor which accompanied the scientific revolution may be caught in the work of La Mettrie on *Man a Machine*.[186] La Mettrie advocated that mankind should discard religious faith and rely on scientific discoveries alone to reveal the laws of nature and of life. But the new truth, thus revealed, was conceived solely in physical, and never in metaphysical, terms. The priesthood of the white coat too often saw the world from a one-dimensional view. Faith, along with feeling, was shunned as subjectivist: The human being was a part of an interacting system of objective laws; the microscope, test-tube and atom-smasher could unlock every secret. In the name of science, many took for granted the basic assumptions from which they worked, and then proceeded to narrow down the larger ideas and smooth out all elements of inconsistency.

As these tendencies hardened into a ruling consensus what prevailed was not truth but a thought-controlling orthodoxy. Method had become king and its rule was absolute. Had not Bacon said that knowledge was power? And what knowledge was worthy of the name that was not science? From this followed a new Commandment: Thou shalt do whatsoever lies in thy power. "I can, therefore I do" was the formula by which to live. Truth could now be simply defined as anything that worked, that is, that was capable of producing results. Newton's Great Machine had degenerated into techniques of manipulation. Instead of setting humanity free, science itself became allied with government and business in the power structure of the Corporate State.

But truth, we remember, is great and will prevail. Now in these closing decades of the second millennium, an increasing number of concerned citizens and social philosophers are beginning to question a dogmatic scientism which ignored the wholeness of truth about humanity (including the humanity of the scientists themselves). Today, the wheel has indeed come full circle. For the growing ranks of those who now decry the fallacies and fictions of the once-vaunted method include more and more scientists. As the astronomer Arthur Eddington pointed out fifty years ago, the content of science is what we put there. Similarly, Werner Heisenberg comments: "We have to remember that what we observe is not nature in itself, but nature exposed to our method of questioning."[187] Polanyi has restored to science its original metaphysical foundation in the classical humanist assumptions regarding the quest for truth. In his view, people cannot participate in discussion unless they believe that there is a truth which all hold as a higher value and which all feel capable of pursuing.[188]

Bohr, another radical thinker among the physical scientists, believed as firmly as the ancient Greek philosophers that knowledge forms a unity; but that, because of the inherent complexity of the universe, there may not simply be one way to observe or understand phenomena.[189] Although one can understand some aspects of the nature of things by measuring and predicting in the classical scientific pattern, other aspects—the orbit of an electron within an atom, for instance—do not respond in a predictable fashion when studied experimentally. In fact, their behavior (the "state of the system") is actually changed by the very process of observation. Expressed in another way, what appear to be contradictory states in physics (seeing light as a wave phenomenon and a particle phenomenon, based on a variety of experiments under different conditions) may all be true if one interprets them in a wider frame of reference. Instead of Either-Or, we have Both-And. Gerald Holton, interpreting Bohr's views on complementarity, has this to say:

> ". . . clarity does not reside in simplification and reduction to a single, directly comprehensible model, but in the exhaustive overlay of different descriptions that incorporate apparently contradictory notions."

Bohr was eager to apply this viewpoint to areas other than physics in order to discover the "great inter-relationships among all areas of knowledge." Thus, apparently irreconcilable viewpoints in other fields (such as the physiology of the individual or the culture of human society) can be reconciled if a larger framework is used. In the case of physiology, one does not have to disprove the idea of man either as a living organism or as a mechanism since both can be used as a basis for complete description.

The major concerns of the new wave of thinking are to reaffirm the unity of knowledge and to relate human values to all topics of inquiry. We say "reaffirm" because there is a mixture in this of old and new. Perhaps there is some point in the fact that Aristotle's treatise on the nature of reality and of knowledge was placed in the collection of his works after the *Physics* and thus happened to be called *Metaphysics*. For many of today's thinkers have rediscovered that the knower and the known are complementary and that there is no objective, external reality to which humanity is or ever could be alien. Einstein himself spent an hour every evening reading aloud in Aeschylus, Sophocles or Thucydides and remarked to a friend: "How can an educated person stay away from the Greeks? I've always been far more interested in them than in science." The conceptual ferment of today is, of course, heightened by the awareness that dehumanization seems to increase with the advances of science-based technology. As a consequence, people are reexamining the assumptions which have underlain our reasoning and the values they embody or exclude.[190] Those in particular who project present trends and speculate about the future are bound to raise anew the basic questions about human life and destiny.[191]

The profoundest truth of all has always lain in humility, in the recognition of how little we know. "In Taoist thinking," Fromm has written, "just as in Indian and Socratic thinking, the highest step to which thought can lead is to know that we do not know. . . . The ultimate reality, the ultimate One, cannot be caught in words or in thoughts."[192] If, therefore, we would seek truth, we first should heed the Delphic Oracle and know ourselves. We will note that we are forked animals, but animals endowed with eyes which can see the distant stars and with insight which can speculate beyond them. We can even see beyond truth—to beauty and to love.

Beauty

Beauty and the arts which express it are central to human existence. They provide at once the *raison d'être* and the *élan vital*. In the Christian era, they were held to purify mankind by bringing us nearer to God. In the Renaissance, when humanity was exalted, they were felt to help individuals find and express their potentialities.

We would not have our guardians reared among
images of evil as in a foul pasture, and there day by
day and little by little gather many impressions
from all that surrounds them, taking them all in until
at last a great mass of evil gathers in their inmost
souls, and they know it not. No, we must seek
out those craftsmen who have the happy gift of tracing
out the nature of the fair and graceful, that our
young men may dwell as in a health-giving region
where all that surrounds them is beneficent,
whencesoever from fair works of art there smite upon
their eyes and ears an affluence like a wind bringing
health from happy regions, which, though they
know it not, leads them from their earliest years into
likeness and friendship and harmony with the
principle of beauty.

Plato, *The Republic*, Book III, Sect. 401, *op. cit.* p. 84.

Throughout most of history they have been seen as transcendental agents. Every person could become a better self either through expressing beauty (in an art form) or through its appreciation (whether in art or in nature). All people in all places at all times have responded to beauty. Not only is it a universal value, as was suggested earlier, but it appeals to the human being's profoundest sensibilities, to the very core of our humanness.

No exact answer can be given to the question of how beauty and art inspire and enhance the human being and at times allow us to transcend ourselves. But some artists and philosophers have offered suggestions as to why this is the case and how it can happen. Tolstoy provided a fundamental insight when he answered the question: What is art for? Art makes men human—"The evolution of feeling proceeds by means of art;" everyone can partake—"art is accessible to all men;" and only art will insure peace on earth—"art and only art can cause violence to be set aside."[193]

Individual growth, as we traced it earlier, passes through many stages. But a most fundamental advance is reached in the develop-

*I believe, and it is belief based on much objective
experimental evidence, that at any given time only a
very small percentage of the genetic endowment
is expressed. Human beings are endowed with a
number of potentialities which are inscribed in
a genetic code. This genetic code of man is active to
only a very small extent in any given time. And
that aspect or part which is active is that which has
been activated by environmental stimuli.*

Interview with René Dubos conducted by Elizabeth Monroe
Drews, October 1967.

---

ment of mind and character when the individual begins to find pattern and form in experience. The human search for meaning begins at birth when the infant confronts this "big blooming buzzing confusion" that William James called the experience of living. One must find some stability in this world of things or one cannot be sane. Dubos, in fact, believes that all human beings, in order to become human as we know or would like to know them, must experience the ambiences of nature—blue skies, fleeting clouds, the shift of seasons, and the flowering of plants.

Art, as well as nature, supplies these patterns. As the buzz becomes a roar and the confusion turns to chaos in the Age of the High Technic, art can offer sanctuary and security. Or beauty as experienced in nature can cushion and enhance the life of everyone. The joy in spring's petals and winter's snowflakes is a universal response of children. These patterns can protect from what Alvin Toffler has called "future shock."[194] They can supply the resources that make it possible for a person to continue on the path of growth toward self-actualization. Interacting with the arts and with nature, we will find that we can begin to give form to all that we make and do. These patterns, both those that shape us as we reach out in appreciation and the ones we ourselves shape through our own creative expression, will increase our assurance and allow us to live at our fullest.

Too much formless matter, too much aimless movement, frustrated effort, and kaleidoscopic wildness, will foster madness—as, on the other hand, will too little complexity and change. The beauty of wild nature can soothe and exalt, particularly if this is enjoyed in the company of loving guides. So, too, can art. Instead of a waking dream, life without art will slip into the shapeless incoherences and nameless horrors of a nightmare. Art, therefore, offers a way out of the wilderness inhabited by the space-age minotaurs. Guided by the artist, the individual can find symmetry in vision and harmony in sound. The world may indeed be absurd, as Camus has said, but we have it in our power to give it order. Camus continually stressed the irrational nature of the world and its fundamental absurdity. He saw the universe as chaotic, as devoid of pattern except what each individual brings to it. Each of us therefore must become responsible for our own acts. All of us have it in ourselves to become autonomous and creative. Taking command of our own lives, we can exercise a conscious choice and thus act on our environment.

To do so is the task of everyman, but more importantly it is the mission of the artist. The latter can give us eyes with which to see and ears with which to hear. As Edith Sitwell sketches the artist's task:

"It is a part of the poet's work to give each man his own view of the world—show him what he sees but does not know that he sees."[195]

In the past, the great artists have taken as their task the shaping of a world, the intimation of a cosmology. Shelley said of his celebrated contemporaries: "They measure the circumference and sound the depths of human nature with a comprehensive and all-penetrating spirit . . . the spirit of the age." Shelley was speaking of the poets of his time, but he also included Raphael and Michelangelo and all great artists. Somehow, such creative geniuses are able to "express what (other men) do not understand." Unwittingly and unacknowledged, they are the "legislators of the world."[196]

Despite the tendency of 20th-century scholars and scientists to see human nature as basically flawed or, at best, as inert protoplasm, many still hold that great art requires ennobling conceptions of mankind.[197] Such conceptions, if they are to be inspiring legislators for the world, must teach mankind to be more generous and human, to live more graciously and joyfully. Artists, like teachers, are communicators. They must be concerned not only with beauty and clarity of expression, but also with the ethics of the message they communicate. On this point Simone Weil has declared unequivocally "that artists must accept responsibility for the kind of influence they exert."[198] No more than the scientific discovery can the aesthetic creation be sent into the world an unattached orphan. Both artist and scientist are responsible for their offspring. Both must be more concerned for mankind than for egocentric activity. The "learning to learn" of the child can all too easily lead to "science for science's sake," "art for art's sake," and eventually "revolution for the hell of it." To be worthy of the name, therefore, the artist must serve and love humanity. Whitman told us how this might come about:

> Now that he has passed that way see after him!
> There is not left any vestige of despair or
> misanthropy or cunning or exclusiveness, or
> the ignominy of a nativity or colour or
> delusion of hell or the necessity of hell;
> and no man thenceforth shall be degraded for
> ignorance or weakness or sin.[199]

The "leading out" or educating, which occurs when beauty is formed and expressed by the artist, serves not only to organize chaos to meet basic security needs, but also to elevate and inspire. Great art speaks out for life and vitality, never for death and depression. Whitehead spoke of the exuberance that was Shakespeare's.[200] Edith Sitwell also singled out as characteristic his love of life:

> "To Shakespeare, only that which was too cold for hell is to be condemned. Only the hard heart offends. He sees the fundamental splendour of all living things."[201]

How different from art are the shriveled fruits of formal education, those products of an ill-tended tree of knowledge which so rarely reveal generosity of spirit! Gandhi said that he was troubled most by the hardness of heart of the educated. At the center of all human insight lie the willingness and capacity to face the important issues: What is life about and how should I go about living it? It is in the great works of literature that we find this richness of mind:

> ". . . in the classics of high religion, the Greek myths and dramas, the Dialogues of Plato, the plays of Shakespeare, and the works of other great poets and writers who forever return us to the fundamental questions of human life."[202]

Now we can appreciate the point made by Read that "Life, in its intimate recesses is intelligence, is creative, is art."[203] He felt the aim of artists and scientists alike should be what Wordsworth called "joy in widest commonality spread." To Read, this meant a "society rid of its neuroses, a civilization rid of the threat of annihilating war" by an active participation in art that could perform "the unique function of uniting men in love of each other and of life itself."[204] Both Tolstoy and Read believed that a true education came through the direct experiencing of art—that the hands must find work, the capacity to perceive form must be exercised, and the human potential be used to its fullest. Otherwise, as Read warned, "in idleness and vacancy we [will] revert to violence and crime. When there is no will to creation, the death instinct takes over and wills endless, gratuitous destruction." This is a view in which Irwin Edman concurs, claiming that beauty makes life meaningful. Art can make "Our relations with others . . . all have something of the quality of friendship and affection. . . ." When that occurs, Edman continues, "Living would be at once ordered and spontaneous, disciplined and free."[205]

There are occasions, however, when art moves away from the function which Shelly, Tolstoy and Read have envisaged. If "the time is out of joint," artists do not always conceive it as their mission "to set it right." Instead, they may be deliberately representational or bloodlessly abstract. They will then depict violence, mirror insanity, portray ugliness or even nothingness. Such themes, of course, are not new in the annals of art. Ugliness and violence were graphically depicted by Breughel, Hogarth, and Goya—to name only a few. But their canvases throb with the feeling of protest against the inhumanities or their times. They label the evil for what it is and plead that we should renounce it. With many of today's artists, however, this is not the case. Too often, theirs is a medium without a message—observe the contemporary trends in much of the painting, sculpture, architecture, and drama. Our civilization, as was suggested before, is thought by many to have gone off the track; our elites appear to be confused; most of our creative youth are alienated; and the "hosannas that they ache to hear"[206] are silent for most.

In the 20th century, as many see it, we have rejected the very values that have made us human. Some Americans even begin to doubt whether we ever had our higher moments. As Georges Clemenceau is reported to have said: "America is the only nation in history which miraculously has gone from barbarism to degeneration without the usual interval of civilization." To this, all too many artists have responded in the spirit of Hamlet's advice to the Players. They choose no longer to ennoble and uplift, but rather to serve as "the abstracts and brief chronicles of the time." Their themes, then, are violence, absurdity, madness, formalism devoid of life, or mere technique substituting for content. They tell us too well about the forces that surface and glower at every turn. Rarely do they conjure up the alternative vision of beauty, tenderness and joy. By neglecting these, they do not fulfill the task of the artist which Shelley and Sitwell defined as telling us what is it that we see unknowingly. This, of course, is the Socratic task of all true teachers—to show us what we already know and, as Polanyi suggests, to help us see that "we know more than we know we know."[207]

Creating beauty is no longer the goal of many artists. Camus believed that mankind could not live without beauty, and he contrasted the ancient Greeks who took up arms on her behalf with the modern Western World which has outlawed her.[208] Art, which at one time existed to fulfill our need for beauty, has now, as Read contends, abandoned its "philosophic guides." He continues:

"This art without concentration, without relationship, this art which boasts of its inconsequence and incoherence, is not art at all, and though some of its practitioners are undoubtedly sensitive they are like delinquent children who destroy a beautiful object shamelessly because they are not loved, because they resent the world they did not make, a darkening world indeed—a world characterized in Heidegger's words by 'the flight of the Gods, the destruction of the earth, the standardization of man, the preeminence of the mediocre.' "[209]

Yet here and there, now and then, there are signs of the rebirth of the tender and a renewed interest in the beautiful. Songs written in the sixties were often hauntingly poignant. Crafts long dormant have been revived by young artisans. Psychedelic patterns and sounds were rounded out by the new multi-media blends. At the end of the decade, these new art forms culminated in *Hair*—improvisational and fluid, combining drama, dance and song in a pulsatingly strident, joyful release. In fact, there is recent evidence that the old values are taking on new importance. Not only the youth, but people of all ages are criticizing the repeated deviations from truth, the subtle and not-so-subtle hypocrisies practised by the average citizen, by the advertisers and the corporations they serve, as well as by the

*There is a land of the living and a land of the
dead and the bridge is love, the only survival, the
only meaning.*

Thornton Wilder, *The Bridge of San Luis Rey*, New York:
Washington Square Press, copyright 1927, 41st printing,
1967. This is the concluding sentence.

---

policy-makers of nation-states. Rejecting substitutes which are flimsy
and tawdry, people not only raise basic questions, but reach out for
joy and beauty.

Increasing numbers of our most gifted youth go beyond questioning the values of the larger society to repudiate the more sterile
modes of knowing. For them, at least, "mere reason is not enough."
To some observers the vibrating melange that contemporary youth
creates is pure chaos. But no one can deny its organic exuberance.
Despite its overtones, it bears a close genealogical resemblance to
what has been called the "poetry of cosmic consciousness,"[210] to the
new physics of indeterminacy, and to the unitive ground of the
perennial philosophy. Severally and together, all of these—the art
forms, the science, and the philosophy—are synergic. "The Sounds
of Silence" are as important as the music that connects them. The
white space speaks as loudly as the brush stroke. Human beings are
unconscionably diverse, but bound together in psychic unity. For
between all men, as Thornton Wilder knew, there is the bridge of
love.

Love

Each of us has a vast, unrealized potential. But encased as we are in
institutions and social roles, we usually lead a life of uneasy sym-
biosis, out of touch with ourselves and with others.[211] Love, however, can provide a bridge between the many selves within the self
and between the self and the others without. Not only is love one of
the trinity of the highest values, flanked by truth and beauty, but for
such of its students as Buber and Sorokin, and for people in general
it is the supreme value.[212] Love is both at the top of the apex of
values and rooted in the solid ground below. It is a basic need that

must be met at the very beginning of life. Mothers seem to know that babies cannot survive without love, and research has documented their knowledge. Maslow has affirmed that "The need for love characterizes every human being that is born."[213] "A being," as Henry Anderson remarks, "becomes human through sympathy."[214] Kenneth Clark observes that every infant needs love, and René Spitz has compiled a vast body of data to show that those deprived of love in early life often do not survive, while those who do will probably be maimed psychologically.[215] Drawing on this and other evidence, Sorokin has assembled facts which indicate that children denied love or, worse yet, abused and treated cruelly, are commonly warped in their psychological growth. Conversely, those who are found to be neurotic, who have character disorders, or who strike out at society through delinquent acts have generally not been loved. Indeed, as Jung states it: "Where love stops, power begins, and violence, and terror."[216]

Love can be seen, then, as a life force absolutely essential for healthy human growth. Simultaneously, it can be viewed in the way that Jesus perceived it, "as the highest manifestation of life."[217] It changes behavior and heightens perceptions. Beauty is enhanced and truth is seen more clearly. Love is momentary perfection, both tinder and spark, the peak experience, which is how Maslow describes it.[218] It may well be, as Goethe suggested, that "we only learn through those we love."

Empirical efforts are sometimes made to measure this elusive but omnipresent quality. Psychologists have documented the amount of attention that mothers give their children, the atmospheres of classrooms, and the attitudes of teachers toward pupils. All these have been placed on a continuum ranging from rejection to acceptance. Undoubtedly psychological insights are gained from these studies; but those who hold the human being to be more than a reactive organism understand that the essence of love cannot be charted. For example, no one can really explain why children love one teacher and learn avidly in her ambience, while another teacher will literally leave them cold. Similarly, to predict who will fall in love with whom is difficult, if not impossible. This is a subject on which some general observations can be made, but exact measurements and sharply defined criteria seem futile. In a way, the dilemma of all scientific attempts to observe love would parallel those reported by physicists who study atomic structure. In their effort to observe the electron, the light they used disturbed it and altered its velocity. But without light, there can be no measurement and therefore no knowledge. Or, as one minor poet has stated the dilemma, less scientifically but with no less insight:

> Love will fly if held too tightly,
> Love will die if held too lightly,
> Lightly, tightly, how do I know
> Whether I'm killing or letting you go?

Despite the inadequacy of objective studies, there is plenty of descriptive literature on altruism and love which can provide guidance in terms of higher orders of human development. Much of this is reported by Sorokin who believes that altruism in the home is the easiest and perhaps the best way to produce the good person. Fromm speaks of motherly love as "unconditional affirmation of the child's life and his needs."[219] This affirmation, he makes clear, has two aspects. One is the care and responsibility which are absolutely necessary for the preservation of the child's life and his growth; and the other is an attitude which allows the child to engage fully with life. Fromm refers to milk as being the symbol of the first aspect of love, that of care and affirmation. Honey symbolizes the second aspect— the sweetness of life and love for it, as well as the sheer happiness in being alive. "Most mothers," in his words "are capable of giving 'milk,' but only a minority of giving 'honey.' " He comments that a child may learn either joy or anxiety from the mother, depending on her dominant attitude. Without absorbing this love for life, it is much harder for the individual to proceed eventually to the higher levels of development or to self-actualization.

After the mother, it is the mature teacher who will be able to carry the child a step further. She can educate in the ancient sense of "leading out." Buber explains how this might be done:

> "It is only when someone takes him by the hand not as a 'creator,' but as a fellow-creature lost in the world, and greets him not as an artist but as comrade, friend or lover, that he experiences an inner reciprocity."[220]

Buber emphasizes that the teacher must care a great deal about the student for the essential relationship ("a constant condition of reciprocity") to develop. It is the teacher's task to think about and bring the student into her imagination, to experience and appreciate the latter's individuality. To do this, she must identify with the child and "feel and do as he does." As growth continues, the teacher learns to distinguish the emerging individuality of each student and anticipate what this particular person "needs in order to become human." Through such a conception of teaching, Buber hopes that it will be possible to overcome "oppositeness." Instead, "the teacher becomes the uniter, the mediator between the individual and his environment, the midwife through whose agency the individual is reborn into society, guided into its most vital currents."

From studying how counselors and teachers can help others become more human, Rogers concludes that it is essential that we value all human beings and think of each, not as a machine or a collection of stimulus-response bonds, and never as an object or a pawn, but rather as a unique individual of unconditional worth. Through such loving guidance, each can become psychologically mature—"a more autonomous, more spontaneous, more confident person."[221]

Jahoda has extensively studied this maturity which she defines as positive mental health. She characterizes its dimensions as self-awareness, self-acceptance, and self-confidence.[222] Fromm, arguing that self-love is a necessary aspect of maturity, believes it to be a logical fallacy "that love for others and love for oneself are mutually exclusive."[223] In addition to being logically fallacious, this belief is also psychologically false. Self-love and love for others can be seen as yet another instance of the complementarity principle. Fromm explains the paradox as follows:

"The idea expressed in the Biblical 'Love thy neighbor as thyself!' implies that respect for one's own integrity and uniqueness, love for and understanding of one's own self, cannot be separated from respect and love and understanding for another individual. The love for my own self is inseparably connected with the love for any other being."[224]

There are many ways, according to Sorokin, in which the individual can discover both his own identity and his bonds of communion with his fellowmen. It is such experiences that annul our individual loneliness and bind us to others. "Love is literally," as Sorokin says, "a *life-giving force.*"[225] It leads to true cognition, it beautifies life, and it allows one to act freely. Buber, too, maintains that beyond the "instinct to originate" there is an "instinct for communion," and he sees the latter as the more important of the two. To be united with our fellowmen or with nature, one must first be free

---

and independent. But "independence is a path and not a dwelling
place. . . . Freedom in education is nothing else but possession of the
ability to be united."[226]

How then can we create the circumstances in which this union is
likely to occur? How can we help people to live together peacefully
and to love one another? How can we diminish hostility and aggression? Beyond the need for a loving mother—the "lucky package" of
a good family—Sorokin maintains that it is desirable for people to
live in a group or "an agency" where altruism is the norm.[227] It was
his finding that most of the great altruistic leaders have emerged
from such groups. Here the young are most likely to discover
"heroes of love" and "athletes of good," and to learn, through them,
how to love. If our youth, or anyone for that matter, are to become
more altruistic and socially concerned, they need inspiring examples
with whom they can identify. It is to these enlightened men and
women, Polanyi says, that we should "entrust ourselves, by trying
to understand their works and to follow their teachings and
examples."[228]

In all situations, Sorokin stresses the therapeutic value of over-
whelming kindness. At any time in his life an individual may turn
away from greed and hostility toward altruistic caring by a deliberate decision or as a result of a transcendent experience. For most
people, this growth of concern for others is apt to occur as a result
of a love relationship. But solitude and retreats, and even such negative events as great tragedies and crises can also be precipitating
forces which change the direction of a life. However, it is only the
unusual person who is apt to profit from tragic or profoundly dis-
rupting experiences. Sorokin remarks about the problems that attend
such experiences: "The more hellish is his total environment, the
lesser are the chances for a . . . crop of truly altruistic persons, even

*We can only love what we know, and we can
never know completely what we do not love. Love is
a mode of knowledge, and when the love is
sufficiently disinterested and sufficiently intense, the
knowledge becomes unitive knowledge.*

Aldous Huxley, *The Perennial Philosophy*, Cleveland: World
publishing Company, Meridian Books, 1962, p. 81.

---

of good neighbors..."[229] Most individuals will respond not with
serenity and compassion, but with inner turmoil—out of which
comes a lowered self-concept or even demoralization. To weather
such psychological storms, to avoid moral and mental disintegration,
one needs a "strong soul"—the very quality required by those whom
Sorokin characterizes as "Unattached Pilgrims of Goodness." Those
who would become effective pilgrims must have "completed self-
identification." It is at this point in development that individuals can
emerge as "free instruments of universal compassion and love."[230]

Granted that it is possible for people to develop in these ways, do
they want to? We cannot deny that many young people today are
seeking to communicate with one another across the bridge of love,
and for this purpose are experimenting with new structures and new
media. One who has expressed this message to millions is Joan Baez.
In discussing her Institute for the Study of Non-Violence she has
this to say:

> "The thing that keeps me doing the things I do and
> makes me think they may work ... is that I've never in my travels
> met a person who didn't want to love and be loved by other people.
> ... That's the force I try to work with. *It's there.*"[231]

Those who are usually classified as the adult population reveal similar feelings through the words they commonly use. For them too
love is the greatest force. On this point, the results of a recent
research study contain important insights. People in general were
found to prefer love over hate and to express this in the words of
everyday speech. The same study revealed, however, that writing
and research of academics—the words they use and the subjects
they choose—emphasize the opposite.[232] Scholarly treatises and text-

books, no matter in what subject area, rarely index the word love. Year after year, senior honor students at a large midwestern university reported that none of their professors had a good word to say about humanity in general and even few accolades for any individual.[233] When today's youth, on the other hand, are so openly votaries of love in their songs, slogans, and life-styles, could this be yet another example of the scholastic irrelevance of academia?

The effects of love or its opposite can be traced in several ways. Sorokin repeatedly affirms that love begets love and hate begets hate. Illustrative parables and aphorisms abound:

> "One touch of kindness makes the whole world kin."
> "There never was a bad peace or a good war."
> "Those who live by the sword, die by the sword."
> "The Revolution devours its children."

Sociological research and current literature contain innumerable allusions to the destructive force of hate. The "Organization S.O.B.'s" who are hired as professional hatchet-men, are nearly always done in by others who use the same weapons.[234] Likewise, James Thurber tells the tale of "Proudfoot, the Tiger," who regularly mauled Mama Tiger and the cubs, but ended up spread-eagled, a resplendent rug on the living room floor.[235]

It is abundantly clear that, as each proliferates, hate casts its blight and love spreads its bloom. Ian Suttie discusses how love can radiate outwards in ever larger concentric circles—moving from parental love for a child to love within the small group, to love within the community, and eventually to the love of all mankind.[236] In order to form such relationships readily with people outside the immediate family, psychologists generally hold that one must have experienced a loving relationship with another mature person. Fromm speaks of "brotherly love" as the most fundamental form of all: "By this, I mean the sense of responsibility, care, respect, knowledge of another human being, the wish to further his life . . . the kind of love the Bible speaks of when it says: Love thy neighbor as thyself." Since it is love for all human beings, brotherly love is in no way exclusive. It is based on the belief that all men are one. This develops into love for the helpless, for the poor, for the stranger, and finally for the enemy. As Fromm concludes: "Only in the love of those who do not serve a purpose, love begins to unfold."[237]

Does all of this matter, some people ask? What difference does it make if one loves and is altruistic? In the first place, as we have already seen, it has some highly practical consequences. Without it, the baby will not survive and those deprived of love lead miserable lives. "The experience of a truly great love," Sorokin affirms, "is the highest form of happiness. . . . It is the *summum bonum*."[238] Those who come from loving homes and have good experiences in school and life tend to live longer, to be healthier and happier. Students who "love" to study for the sheer pleasure of searching for truth, who feel that their teachers like them, are generally happier and live longer than those who find school a hard grind. Carlson discovered that honor graduates of middle western universities lived the longest of all groups he studied.[239] Maslow reports that self-actualizing optimists are healthier and probably longer lived than other people. In his words,

> "It's certainly true that within our own area of the psychosomatic, workers have taught us that people who are happy, people who are optimistic are simply more resistant to disease. They just live longer."[240]

Sorokin's research on over 3500 Christian saints shows "that they had notably longer life duration than their unsaintly and less altruistic contemporaries."[241] And this without discounting the fact that 37 per cent of them were prematurely killed by their persecutors!

For love to prevail generally in human relationships—to become the rule rather than the exception—there is a need for radical change either in our thought patterns or our conduct, or in both. Our conduct may be wrong either because we pay lip service to the higher values but depart from them in practice, or because the practice is based on and conforms to such lower social values as expediency, conspicuous consumption and status, or to the assumed biological imperatives of aggression, egotism and competition.

There seems to be no reason to disagree with Fromm that even "in the industrial society, the official, conscious values are those of the religious and humanistic tradition: individuality, love, compassion, hope, etc."[242] However most people, even those who subscribe to these values, do not live by them, at least in their public lives. And there is much evidence that this kind of hypocrisy, even though it is unconscious, contributes to the general malaise. "Truth is to be lived, it is not to be merely pronounced with the mouth. . . ."[243] Others in this age of value confusion have eschewed not only the behavior but the values as well. They openly support the social "values" and the biological imperatives over the traditional values. To them—if they had ears to hear—should be voiced the ancient apostolic injunction: "And be ye not conformed to this world: but be ye transformed by the renewing of your mind."[244]

Why do principle and practice so rarely coincide and why do so many people choose the lower values? Is there some weakness in human thinking that distorts and limits our actions? Perhaps, as Shakespeare suggests, "The fault . . . is not in our stars, but in ourselves."[245] Many scholars and philosophers who have reflected on the human condition have concluded that our image of mankind, despite our possession of almost unlimited capacities, is all too often negative and self-limiting. Mumford reminds us that

> "The 'belief' that the world was flat was once upon a time more important than the 'fact' that it was round; and that belief kept the sailors of the medieval world from wandering out of sight of land as effectively as would a string of gunboats or floating mines."[246]

Similarly people who are convinced that they are bad animals, and that this is a fact of life will live by this belief. Ignoring the body of evidence that our species is basically good and has a great capacity to grow in transcendent ways, they remain far below their potential —captives of their own misconceptions rather than "masters of their fates" and "captains of their souls."

Although the common man cannot see that his potential might extend beyond limited horizons and fears the monsters that lie beyond his ken, there is evidence that even the most ordinary person has great unused ability.[247] As Julian Huxley holds, "man is still very much an unfinished type, who clearly has actualized only a small fraction of his potentialities."[248] The biologist, N. J. Berrill, sees our species as just beginning to be human. It is his view that the real trouble is not that we are human, but that we are not human enough. To the question: What does it mean to be human? he answers that it means to be youthful and zestful in spirit, a quality which makes some people more human than others. It is a freshness and eagerness of mind that stays with the lucky ones all of their lives.[249] However, it is possible that such a self-image of joy and confidence may never develop due to personal fears. Too often the self-concept is warped or limited because those with whom the individual interacts judge him or her—and perhaps themselves and all humanity—as basically evil or as formless matter to be manipulated at will.

If we do have this vast potential but use very little of it, as those

He who has never loved, has never felt the call
of a heroic ethic—to give and not to count the cost,
to labor and not to ask for any reward—has lived
far below the peak levels of human experience.

Kenneth Boulding, *Beyond Economics*, Ann Arbor: University
of Michigan Press, 1968, p. 218.

---

who study human potentialities contend, are we beginning to understand why? Do hopelessness and pessimism spring from a belief that
one is at heart a "bad animal" or a powerless bit of flotsam and jet-
sam? If we are constrained by negative images, by fear and self-
doubt, will positive images, hope and confidence, bring us release?
How can all of us learn to work with our strengths, to rejoice in and
develop our potential? How can we reach out to and love our fellowmen? We have suggested this might be achieved through an expansion of self-awareness, a new vision of man, a cosmic consciousness.
Aldous Huxley has said:

"It is because we don't know who we are, because we
are unaware that the Kingdom of Heaven is within us, that we
behave in the generally silly, the often insane, the sometimes criminal
ways that are so characteristically human. We are saved, we are liberated and enlightened, by perceiving the hitherto unperceived good
that is already within us. . . ."[250]

In the late 1960s several movements developed in American society which were attempted correctives for "lives of quiet desperation." Among these were a rising concern for community (accompanied by the creation of communes, both formal and informal), a
reaching out toward the insights of the Eastern mystics coupled with
a renewed interest in meditation, and all the variations on the human
potential theme—"T-groups," sensitivity training, encounters, and
so on. Many advocated, as did Rousseau and Thoreau, the simple
life and a return to nature. They searched for meaning, for affirmation, for joy, for serenity. We cannot yet know which, if any, of
these explorations will be effective. But these seems to be no doubt
that these are just the early intimations of a massive search which
may embrace all mankind in the future. The styles are peculiarly
contemporary but the themes are old ones. The latter are reaffirmations of the eternal verites—in particular the highest value, love.

Behind all beneficial relationships, love is the animating principle. In truth, it is their breath of life (in Latin the word *anima* refers to the principle of life). Without love, the truth that "all men are created equal" will not be realized, nor can justice emerge or liberty survive. Without love, groups, schools, and housing projects can never be integrated except in formal terms. True integration and communion will not be realized unless there is the bond of love. Otherwise, the classroom or the house will be divided against itself. And divided it will remain, unless we shift the priorities in our thinking from the competitive to the cooperative, unless love becomes truly unselfish and not a technique for barter, unless we are prepared to give without counting the cost. Only when we cease to see others as rivals can we rejoice in their triumphs or their goodness. And as Emerson remarked, if no one had to take the credit, there would be no limit to what we could do.

All that Aldous Huxley called disinterestedness—including those qualities of charity and humility[251] which are the opposite of self-aggrandizement and aggression—expresses that kind of love which realizes itself in the service of others. Too rarely have people been able to achieve the harmonious balance which Whitman celebrated in his verse and in his philosophy, combining, as he did, the "song of myself" with a joyous love for his fellowmen:

> The world, the race, the soul—in
>   space and time the universes,
> All bound as is befitting each—all
>   surely going somewhere.

Similarly, few have been able to follow Emerson's suggestion that they be self-reliant while at the same time reaching deeply for friendship and love. Nor have many achieved the wholeness and integrity in their lives that he achieved in his. These two philosopher-poets, as Mumford said, were more able than most to extend the teachings of Jesus.[252] The same could be said of a Florence Nightingale, a Jane Addams, or an Eleanor Roosevelt. If mankind's future is to be better than the past, those few must become not only known but numerous. It is men and women such as these who can provide a guiding vision for many today and for multitudes tomorrow.

CHAPTER EIGHT

Conclusions

There is much evidence to show that people in general are unhappy. This is true not only of those groups against whom the prevailing system discriminates, but also of many to whom its opportunities and rewards are fully accessible. Alienation is widespread among the youth, as every teacher knows, and also among a large number of the highly educated adults. Violence accelerates continually; and the very governments, which condemn it in the untrained and usually unarmed individual, themselves foster it at the hands of the armed aggregate.

For more than a century, in the culture of the West and in its off-shoots and imitators elsewhere, science has been applied to technology, the economy has been industrialized, and our social system, growing ever more complex, has been bureaucratically managed through large organizations. We can now see that this has not resulted in an increase of good feelings or a closer sense of community. On the contrary, one detects in the climate of today an atmosphere of doubt, a loss of confidence, an awareness that our civilization is not functioning well. This pervasive uncertainty is reflected in the lack of self-confidence—literally the failure of nerve—on the part of many individuals. For many there is no clear understanding of why this is so. Our question has been: How can we better understand the situation? We have seen that social philosophers, most creative intellectuals, large numbers of the young, and many ordinary people, are now sensing that there must be something wrong with the values by which we live. If it is true, as Maslow said, that we human beings need values just as we need food and calcium, and that it is the higher values which are the most apt to contribute to a happier and more self-actualizing person, then how can people come to understand what it is they need? How can those trends which are working to humanity's disadvantage be arrested so that all of us can become our best selves?

This is why we believe that the discussion of values, and the hierarchy they form, is so important. If we need to take soundings, locate our position and then journey on, the highest values can help us find the route. Paradoxically, it is a route which points both forward and backward. These dreams of something better which people so frequently express today are a blend of nostalgia and novelty. There are in them the elements of conservatism and radicalism. Truth, beauty, and love are reaffirmations of values which have been a part of our cultural heritage for more than two millennia. For that reason, and because they correspond to universal aspects of human nature, we speak of them as the eternal verities. But these same ideals are in need of continuous revitalizing. Each new generation, each person, has to rediscover them. They must be reinterpreted in the context of the present as well as for the shaping of the future, for they are dynamic, open-ended, and infinite.

With each passing year, it becomes more clearly apparent that we have entered the era of a revolution whose central concern is to formulate anew the values by which we can live better lives. Mankind stands on the threshold of a great leap into a time of uncharted possibilities. Since what we are is what we think about and want to be, our destiny is ours to make. We can become whatever we want.

It is because of the divergence between our ideals and our practices, because many have discarded the higher human values under the exigencies of modern life, that we ask these questions: Where have we gone wrong? How can we help the good person and the good society to emerge? What steps should we take from here to there?

If the existing social order is now working to the disadvantage of the human and natural worlds, it would seem wise to try something different. Perhaps there is a point in Shaw's reply to the question of what he thought about the Golden Rule: "I can't say. It's never been tried." Similarly, Gandhi answered when someone sought his opinion of western civilization: "I think it would be a good idea." In fact, we know a great deal about the unfavorable effects on human beings of a bad and distorting environment because these have been extensively studied. Much less attention has been paid to the favorable effects of a good environment.

To be realistic, we must recognize that we can only begin at the place where we are now. Hence, as Mumford writes: "This is the first step out of the present impasse: we must return to the real world, and face it, and survey it in its complicated totality. Our castles-in-air must have their foundations in solid ground."[253] For example, it is unrealistic to suppose that we could put a stop to all further technological invention. But it would seem reasonable to slow down the rate of technological change, to plan more carefully for future changes, and to ensure that whatever machines we use should work for humanity's best interests and not the opposite. This is what is required by that enduring and fundamental reality, the law of nature. But such actions lead to this paradox: only by the most idealistic of thinking can we come to grips with these realities. Platt has asserted: "The world is too dangerous for anything short of utopia."[254] Unless, therefore, we fundamentally revise our ways of thinking, feeling, and behaving, we are more likely to be destroyed than saved.

To begin with, we shall need—we must develop—different kinds of education. There is an untapped reservoir of human talent, even of genius, available. When Aldous Huxley says that "the capacities of the human mind are almost infinitely great," this is not a naively visionary statement.[255] It is sober realism. Not only does each person have untold and undeveloped capacities, but even among those who early show themselves to be unusually gifted, and are thus well on the way toward being more fully human, only a few emerge in the ranks of recognized genius. The rest of mankind lose their true selves in the vast sea of mass culture. All young children unquestionably could develop sensitivities and capacities that are largely unknown and at very much faster rates than is now customary. This would be true if we encouraged them to learn at their own pace and in their own style and to follow their own interests as these unfold. Our systems of education might be designed to allow this talent to emerge, to foster and encourage it.

We must educate for empathy, compassion, trust,
non-exploitiveness, non-manipulativeness, for
self-growth and self-esteem, for tolerance of ambiguity,
for acknowledgment of error, for patience, for
suffering.

Donald Michael, *The Unprepared Society: Planning for a*
Precarious Future, New York: Harper Colophon Books, 1970,
p. 109. By permission of Basic Books, Inc., Publishers,
New York, 1968.

Nowadays, too much of what is called education does the reverse. Instead of freeing, it constricts and regiments; instead of encouraging integrative thought, it parcels out bits of knowledge called "facts" and subdivides large subjects (or disciplines) into small, specialized segments. It largely neglects the universal need for beauty and for love and presents only a narrow band of knowledge as if it were the whole truth. Students would undoubtedly find more meaning in their lives, if, in addition to facts and objective data, they were helped to discover patterns of thought (such as the new physics and the new linguistics) which stress the unity of knowledge and of humanity. And they would be more able to find their better selves—become "strong souls" in the Sorokin sense—if they experienced the life-giving force of love. They must be introduced to what Rollo May has called "the mythos of care." This, he has written, "enables us to stand against the cynicism and apathy which are the psychological illnesses of our day."[256] Camus conveys the same message in *The Stranger* when the young Algerian, who does not care enough to cry at his mother's funeral, later realizes that this lack of caring brought on his own destruction.

Donald Michael has written cogently about the kind of education we could have. The concepts presented and the experiences provided would introduce the students to both community and cosmos, so they could feel themselves part of "the total interrelationship of things." They can then grasp the meaning of Francis Thompson's insight:

> Thou canst not stir a flower
> without troubling of a star.[257]

Such thinking and feelings are necessary if the young are to discern the coherence in the complex world around them and relate themselves organically to its natural order. Thus in the cognitive sphere, whether in teaching or in private reflection, we should search for a higher synthesis in order to embrace wider areas of experience. But this must be done without the hubris or heavy-handedness which accompany so much of our professional expertise today. This is pointed out by Watson Thomson, who spent much of his life experimenting with communal patterns of living. "Western man," he remarks, "has been called Faustian or Promethean precisely because of his bias toward this cosmic arrogance, his tendency to think that his powers are limitless."[258] Teaching should be the whisper of suggestion, not the shout of command. For the wisdom which recognizes how little one knows communicates at its best both charity and humility.

So, too, in the aesthetic sphere, it is fitting to tell the artists that they have overplayed the role of holding up a mirror to the sickness of society, since this morbid preoccupation with the perverse and the absurd sets up a reciprocity of negative images. Could not the artists, without explicitly moralizing or being overly didactic, inaugurate the substitution of virtuous circles for vicious? Could they not help us to uncover the significance that resides in the world of nature and of organic forms? Could they not communicate the good through the sensuous appreciation of the beautiful? Could they not join with Whitman in the celebration of life instead of focusing, as is so often done, on disease and death?

The need for aesthetic development is paralleled by what the affective side of our nature demands. St. Augustine's question, "What else is the state but a great robber band if it be lacking in justice?" could be adapted to read: What else is society but a chaotic collection of individuals if it be lacking in love? For every occasion when someone praises the virtues of cooperation, we hear ten times about the advantages of competition. Similarly, appeals to egoism vastly outnumber those to altruism; and bigness and complexity rate higher than smallness and simplicity. Urged so often to assert our individuality and "get ahead," the price we have paid is the sacrifice of community and the loss of truth. Others appear as rivals, then as threats, and thence as enemies. What we need, of course, is to see both individuals and community in complementary terms. How is this possible? Since our mental images influence our action, everything in our relations with others depends on the character of the initial assumptions from which our thinking and our behavior proceed.

Let us assume with Hobbes that we are fundamentally bad animals, or with Locke that each begins life as a blank sheet. What follows? One implication is that the human species is dangerous. Our instincts and passions have evil consequences since we are driven to seek power over others in order to keep them from harming us. Fear, distrust, and suspicion are the maxims of prudence. Since others are by definition antagonistic, only by a sense of self-interest, by stratagem and surprise, will a person survive. For those who accept this Hobbesian premise, life becomes a succession of expedients for the postponement of death. Society, being the alternative to the war of every man against every man, must be organized to bridle the beast. Governments will mobilize the force of Leviathan to apply coercion from without. Education will supplement them by caging the mind, thus implanting the coercion within—the new totalitarianism of mind control. Aldous Huxley characterized all this as consisting of the techniques "which might be used by rulers for keeping their subjects in order and even loving their servitude."[259]

But, what are the consequences that follow from the Lockean assumption that mankind in general is malleable clay awaiting the potter's art? To those who are certain they know best, such an image is an open invitation to mold the soft materials into whatsoever form they will. If the hand be that of a Jefferson, Gandhi, or Jane Addams, the results might be good. Could it have been with such men in mind that Skinner put Frazier at the wheel in *Walden Two*? But suppose the potter is the Great Khan, a Hitler, or a Stalin? Can Lockean Man avoid subjection to the authoritarian ruler? Can the ruler avoid Lord Acton's axiom—that corruption follows from assumed omniscience and absolute power? How can we protect ourselves from those who assume the role of "betters," but who, upon analysis, turn out to be simply more powerful? Sorokin's research, which is very much to the point, demonstrated that those in power are ordinarily less good than their fellowmen.

What is clear about all assumptions based on the negative images of humanity is that they hold out scant prospect of improvement. "You can't change human nature," is what the pessimists reiterate. We can be trapped by whatever image we hold—whether it is fostered through doctrines of "original sin" or the "biological imperative," or simply through the incremental conditioning of the trainer or the Black Box. We can come to see ourselves as evil and fear the "id" inside; or else we can become "dumb animals" who look outside instead of within to find the direction to go and what to do. As the victims of conditioning contentedly intone, "I'm glad I am a gamma because the alphas have to work so hard."

Those, however, who start with the most positive image can conceive of alternatives which are vastly different. Their beliefs will be founded on a faith in human goodness. Education they envisage as creative growth—its goal being autonomy, its method, spontaneity. Their view is holistic. They affirm the unity of all, and the cosmic consciousness which apprehends it. They prize the individuality which is attained through community. Each person they regard as both a unique entity and a part of the universal order.

The self-actualizing individuals, who would emerge ideally from such conceptions as these, are distinguished by many qualities which have been best described by Maslow. Their creative imagination impels them to innovate, while energy, enthusiasm, and peak experiences, flow forth from their exuberant joy in living. Being psychologically healthy, they revel in the exercise of stretching their spiritual muscles. For them, work is not drudgery, but excitement; perseverance is not pain, but a vital force. Tolerant of diversity, they seek to include all differences in the unity of knowledge. Open to the world, and large and generous in spirit, they are able to resist the pressures to conform; and, although supremely sure of their own gifts, their awareness that the universe always will remain essentially a mystery endows them with true humility.

All this is an ideal which we may approximate, but can never wholly realize. Its value is that it provides us with a direction to grow and a model by which to evaluate our growth. Such a state of mind and level of character development is the resource which will allow us to try to change both ourselves and the world for the better. In no way does this conception of the ideal negate or prevent the need to be skeptical and critical of the problems which each of us faces in society—the seductions of creature comforts and the stringent pressures to conform to the social fiction.

According to this philosophy, it is because we are human that we can think in these ways and make such choices. And the choices are of our willing. If things are indeed in the saddle and ride mankind, is is not we ourselves who invited them there? By and large, the obstacles are mainly in our minds which keep the majority of the human race mired down in the Slough of Despond when we could be attempting the ascent to utopia. Primarily, these obstacles are the products of our own faulty images and of the bad habits to which these give rise. Surely, the implication is that, if we want "the relief of Man's estate," we should recognize that the power to improve matters lies within ourselves.

The way to begin is to change our expectations and our images. There are many ways to go about this. The initiative, instead of coming from the charismatic leader as so often in the past, will develop as the collective product of small groups of persons who will respect one another's individuality. The higher social sensitivity of women will have more of an influence than heretofore. And by uniting the cognitive, the aesthetic and the affective into an integrated whole, more people will rise to higher levels of consciousness. Bucke wrote at the turn of the century that we could evolve from simple consciousness to self-consciousness and finally to "cosmic consciousness."[260] It is at this final level that each person would become one with all. At mid-century, Teilhard de Chardin projected the possibility of "universal man,"[261] and still more recently Platt has described how human beings might take "the step to Man."[262] For that step to occur, people must become aware of the potential within, whether this be conceived in the genetic terms which Dubos has described, or in the power of the "collective unconscious," as Jung suggested, or in a more spiritual interpretation—the discovery of an inner peace and tranquility which the Quakers call the "Inward Light." All involve the unfolding, and often the conscious perception, of that which was unperceived but "already within us."[263]

The Chinese have a saying that a journey of a thousand miles begins with a single step. If so, each of us can begin the quest for a better self and a better world with a single act. Reflecting on the scientific study of the physical world, Eddington observed:

>"We have found a strange footprint on the shores of the unknown. We have devised profound theories, one after the other, to account for its origin. At last, we have succeeded in reconstructing the creature that made the footprint. And lo! it is our own."[264]

Can there be any question as to the direction in which we want our footprints to point?

Notes

Introduction

1. Abraham H. Maslow, "A Theory of Metamotivation: The Biological Rooting of the Value-Life," *Journal of Humanistic Psychology*, Fall 1967, pp. 93–127.

2. Erich Fromm, "Values, Psychology, and Human Existence," in Abraham H. Maslow (ed.), *New Knowledge in Human Values*, Harper & Bros., New York, 1959, p. 151.

3. Michael Polanyi, *Personal Knowledge*, University of Chicago Press, 1958.

4. *Republic*, Book VII, sections 534 ff.

5. Matthew Arnold is thus quoted in Louis Untermeyer, *Lives of the Poets*, Simon and Schuster, New York, 1959, p. 251.

6. Northrop Frye, *The Educated Imagination*, Indiana University Press, Bloomington, 1964.

Chapter one

7. Thucydides, *History of the Peloponnesian War*, Book VI, sections 85–111.

8. *Op cit.*, Book I, sections 336–51.

9. *The Prince*, Chapter XVIII.

10. From the second book of Calvin's *Institutes of the Christian Religion*. Quoted by Robert Coles in *The New Yorker* for January 3, 1970, p. 63.

11. Thomas Hobbes, *Leviathan*, Chapter XI.

12. *Ibid.*

13. From Schopenhauer's *Parerga und Paralipomena* (1851) under the heading of "Parables."

14. Quoted by Karen Horney, *New Ways in Psychoanalysis*, W. W. Norton and Co., Inc., New York, 1939, pp. 125–26.

15. *Ibid.*, p. 126.

16. Abraham Maslow, *Toward a Psychology of Being*, Von Nostrand, New York, 2nd ed., 1968, p. 5.

17. John Locke, *Essay on the Human Understanding*, Book II, Chapter I, section 2.

18. Quoted by Floyd W. Matson, *The Broken Image*, Doubleday Anchor Books, New York, 1966, p. 40.

19. Quoted in an article by Sydney Liu in the *San Francisco Sunday Examiner and Chronicle*, December 21, 1969.

20. See Franz Cumont, *The Oriental Religions in Roman Paganism*, Chicago, 1911.

21. Hermann Hesse, *Steppenwolf*, Bantam Books, New York, 1969, pp. 47–48.

22. Erich Fromm, *The Heart of Man*, Harper and Row, New York, 1964, p. 120.

23. For Condorcet's views, see Chapter Six, pp. 94–95.

24. Appendix to Jean-Jacques Rousseau, *Discourse on the Origin of Inequality*, Everyman Edition, p. 239.

25. Quoted by Vernon L. Parrington, *Main Currents in American Thought*, Harcourt, Brace, Jovanovich, Inc., New York, 1927, p. 336, from Moncure D. Conway, *Life of Thomas Paine*, Putnam, 1892–1893, Vol. II, p. 4. Paine made this statement in an address to the French Assembly.

26. The quotation is from a letter to Peter Carr, written in Paris on August 10, 1787. From *The Life and Selected Writings of Thomas Jefferson*, edited by Adrienne Koch and William Peden; Random House, Modern Library, New York, 1944, pp. 430–31.

27. The first quotation is from "Minor Prophecies", section B, "There is no Natural Religion," p. 100. The second is from "The Marriage of Heaven and Hell," p. 129. Both of the above selections are from *Selected Poetry and Prose of William Blake*, Northrop Frye, (ed.), Random House, Modern Library, New York, 1953.

28. These statements of Emerson are from "The Transcendentalists," in the first series of essays. See the Modern Library edition of *The Complete Essays and Other Writings of Ralph Waldo Emerson*, (Brooks Atkinson, ed.), Random House, New York, 1940, p. 90.

29. *Ibid.*, p. 95.

30. J. A. Froude, *Inaugural Lecture at St. Andrew's University*, 1869, p. 41. Quoted in Ralph Barton Perry, *General Theory of Value*, Longman's Green and Co., New York, 1926, p. 128.

31. Thomas Carlyle, in a letter to Froude, *Longman's Magazine*, 1892, p. 151. Quoted in Perry, *Ibid.*

32. Thomas Hobbes, *Leviathan*, Part I, Chapter VI.

33. See Chapter Five, pp. 73 ff.

34. Leopold von Wiese and Howard Becker, *Systematic Sociology*, John Wylie and Sons, New York, 1932, p. 8.

35. Emerson, Essay on the Over-Soul, *op. cit.* p. 262.

36. Samuel Alexander, *Space, Time and Deity*, Macmillan, New York, 1920, Vol. II, p. 302. Quoted in Perry, *op. cit.*, p. 119.

37. Wolfgang Kohler, *The Place of Value in a World of Fact*, Liveright, New York, 1938, pp. 31, 52. The phrasing that "the situation cries out for remedy" was used by Kohler during a public discussion with a philosopher of the positivist school at Swarthmore College in 1948.

38. John Dewey, *Experience and Education*, Macmillan, New York, 1953. The quotations are from Chapters I and V.

39. Dewey, *Freedom and Culture*, G. P. Putnam, New York 1939, p. 175.

40. Lewis Mumford, *The Golden Day*, W. W. Norton & Co., New York, first published in 1926, Chapter III.

41. See *Daedalus* on "Utopia," Vol. 94, Spring 1965.

42. James T. Laney, "The New Morality and the Religious Communities," in *Annals of the American Academy of Political and Social Science*, "The Sixties: Radical Change in American Religion," Vol. 387, January 1970, pp. 14–21.

43. Peter Schrag, writing in *Saturday Review*, (February 18, 1967), named Edgar Friedenberg, Paul Goodman, Jules Henry and John Holt, as "education's new romantic critics." Since his article was written, their group has been greatly augmented.

44. Bohr's complementarity principle is well discussed by Floyd W. Matson in *The Broken Image*, Doubleday Anchor, New York, 1966, pp. 132 ff. For his intellectual biography, see the article by Gerald Holton on "The Roots of Complementarity," in *Daedalus* on "Making of Modern Science: Biographical Studies," Fall 1970, pp. 1015–55, and Ruth Moore, *Niels Bohr*, Knopf, New York, 1966.

45. James Jeans, *The Mysterious Universe*, Dutton & Co. New York, 1958, p. 181.

46. This is Marshall McLuhan's argument in *The Gutenberg Galaxy*, University of Toronto Press, Toronto, 1967.

47. From Thomas B. Colwell, Jr., "The Balance of Nature: A Ground for Human Values," *Main Currents in Modern Thought*, Vol. 26, No. 2, November–December 1969, p. 50.

48. The source is Philip Kapleau, *The Three Pillars of Zen*, John Weatherhill, New York and Tokyo, 1965, p. 154.

Chapter three

49. René Dubos, "Humanistic Biology," *The American Scholar*, Vol. 34, Spring 1965, pp. 179–98.

50. William James, "Energies of Man: excerpts from memories and studies with comments," *Vogue*, Vol. 153, January 1, 1969, pp. 126–29.

51. Paul Goodman, "The Present Moment in Education," *New York Review of Books*, April 10, 1969, pp. 13–24. Elsewhere, he cites James Coleman's opinion "that the average adolescent is really in school, academically, for about ten minutes a day." (See Paul Goodman, *Compulsory Mis-Education*, Horizon Press, New York, 1964, p. 90.)

52. Herbert Read, *Education Through Art*, Faber and Faber, London 1963.

53. William Wordsworth, *Intimations of Immortality from Recollections of Early Childhood*.

54. Sidney M. Jourard, *The Transparent Self*, Van Nostrand, Princeton, N.J., 1964, p. 105.

55. Joseph Wood Krutch, "The Creative Dilemma: It is From the Artist that Society Gains its Loftier Images of Itself," *Saturday Review*, February 8, 1964, pp. 14–17, 58.

56. R. E. Egner and L. E. Denonn (eds.), *The Basic Writings of Bertrand Russell*, Simon and Schuster, New York, 1961.

57. Morris Ginsberg, "On the Diversity of Morals," from his *Essays in Sociology and Social Philosophy*, Penguin Books, Harmondsworth, England, 1968. The reference to Edward W. Westermarck is from *Ethical Relativity*, Kegan & Paul, London, 1932, p. 197.

58. Clyde Klockhohn, *Culture and Behavior*, Richard Kluckhohn, ed., The Free Press, New York, 1962, p. 294.

59. Lawrence Kohlberg, "The Child as a Moral Philosopher," *Psychology Today*, September, 1968, pp. 25–30.

60. Norman Kiell, *The Universal Experience of Adolescence*, Beacon Press, Boston, 1967, p. 40.

61. The *Life* poll by Louis Harris, "What People Think About Their High Schools," *Life Magazine*, May 16, 1969, pp. 22–39.

62. Ralph Barton Perry, *The Humanity of Man*, George Braziller, Inc., New York, 1956, p. 99. Copyright © 1956 by Ralph Barton Perry.

63. Jules Henry, *Culture Against Man*, Random House, New York, 1963, p. 303.

64. Maslow in *Motivation and Personality*, Harper and Bros., New York, 1954. The quotations are from pp. 231 and 210, respectively.

65. On this subject, see Elizabeth Monroe Drews, *The Creative Intellectual Style in Gifted Adolescents*, Vols. I, II, and III, Michigan State University, Lansing, 1964, 1965, 1966.

66. Laing is thus quoted in a *Time* Essay, "Metaphysician of Madness," February 7, 1969, pp. 64–65. See also Ronald D. Laing, *The Politics of Experience* and *The Bird of Paradise*, Penguin Books, Baltimore, 1967.

67. John Martin Rich, *Education and Human Values*, Addison-Wesley Co., Reading, Mass., 1968, p. 111.

68. A. S. Neill, "Can I Come to Summerhill? I Hate My School," *Psychology Today*, May, 1968, pp. 35–40. Also Emmanuel Bernstein, "Summerhill: A Follow-Up of Its Students," *Journal of Humanistic Psychology*, Vol. 8, No. 10, Fall 1968, pp. 123–36.

69. Ashley Montagu, *The Human Revolution*, The World Publishing Co., Cleveland, 1965.

70. Willard Price, *Japan's Islands of Mystery*, John Day, New York, 1944.

71. Robert Lowie, *Are We Civilized?* Harcourt, Brace & Co., New York, 1929, p. 167.

72. Robert Ardrey, *African Genesis*, Atheneum, New York, 1963, pp. 316, 348. His hypotheses are further developed in *The Territorial Imperative*, Atheneum, New York, 1966.

73. W. C. Allee, *Cooperation Among Animals*, Henry Schuman, New York, 1951, p. 206.

74. Sally Carrighar, "War Is Not in Our Genes," *The New York Times Magazine*, October 22, 1967, p. 74.

75. Quoted in Louise Bachelder, ed., *Nature Thoughts*, Peter Pauper Press, Mount Vernon, New York, 1965, p. 34.

76. Aeschylus, *Prometheus Bound*, 11, pp. 88–92. Translated by Leslie Lipson.

77. William Shakespeare, *As You Like It*, II. 1. 3–4.

78. Emerson, Essay on Nature, *op. cit.*, p. 7.

79. William Cullen Bryant, quoted in Bachelder, *op. cit.*, p. 7.

80. John Muir, *ibid.*, p. 23.

81. *Ibid.*, p. 7, for Ruskin; *ibid.*, p. 58, for Muir.

82. *Notes on Virginia*, Query XIX. Similarly, Virgil had written seventeen centuries earlier, in the *Georgics*, that, when Justice departed from the earth, she walked last of all among the tillers of the soil.

83. *The Complete Journal of Townsend Harris*, with introduction and notes by Mario E. Cosenza, Doubleday, New York, 1930, p. 360.

84. Heinrich Engel, *The Japanese House*, Charles E. Tuttle Co., Tokyo, 1964, p. 284.

85. Albert Camus, *The Myth of Sisyphus*, Random House, Vintage Books, New York, 1955, p. 137.

86. Irvin L. Child, "The Experts and the Bridge of Judgment that Crosses Every Cultural Gap," *Psychology Today*, December 1968, pp. 25–29.

87. Dewey, *Art as Experience*, Putnam's Capricorn Books, New York, 1958, p. 329.

88. *Ibid.*, p. 30. The passage from Shelley is quoted by Dewey, *ibid.*, p. 349.

89. See Edward T. Hall, *The Hidden Dimension*, Doubleday, New York, 1966, pp. 58, 143.

90. Read, *op. cit.*; the quotations are from pp. 16, 193.

91. Dewey, *op. cit.*, quoted from pp. 326, 348.

Chapter four

92. Marie Jahoda, *Current Concepts of Positive Mental Health*, Basic Books Publishing Co., Inc., New York, 1958.

93. Jane Loevinger, "The Meaning and Measurement of Ego Development," *American Psychologist*, March 1966, pp. 195–206.

94. Kohlberg, *op. cit.*

95. Claire W. Graves, *On the Theory of Value*, Working Paper, Union College, Schenectady, New York, March, 1967.

96. Robert F. Peck and Robert J. Havighurst, *The Psychology of Character Development*, John Wiley and Sons, New York, 1960.

97. Elizabeth Monroe Drews, *The Creative Intellectual Style in Gifted Adolescents, op. cit.*

98. Maslow, *Toward a Psychology of Being*, 2nd ed., *op. cit.*

99. Carl R. Rogers, *On Becoming a Person*, Houghton-Mifflin Co., Boston, 1961.

100. Mumford, *The Transformations of Man*, Collier Books, New York, 1962, p. 246.

101. Aldous Huxley, *Island*, Harper and Bros., New York, 1962.

102. Teilhard de Chardin, *The Phenomenon of Man*, Harper and Bros., New York, 1959.

103. Polanyi, *Personal Knowledge, op. cit.*

104. John E. Arnold, "The Specialist vs. the Generalist: Productivity vs. Creativity," in Institute for Personality Assessment and Research, *Proceedings of the Conference of the Creative Person*, Lake Tahoe, California, October 13, 1961, pp. 9-I to 9-XIII.

105. Erich Fromm, *Man for Himself*, Rinehart & Co., New York, 1947.

106. Catherine Roberts, *The Scientific Conscience*, George Braziller, Inc., New York, 1967, p. 26. Copyright © 1967 by Catherine Roberts. The meaning of *Arete* is goodness or virtue.

107. Richard M. Bucke, *Cosmic Consciousness*, E. P. Dutton, New York, original copyright 1901, 19th edition, 1959.

108. See Jules Henry, *op. cit.*, p. 319, and Jerome Bruner, *On Knowing: Essays for the Left Hand*, Harvard University Press, Cambridge, 1962, p. 119.

109. Kohlberg, *op. cit.*, p. 26.

110. Loevinger, *op. cit.*

111. Kohlberg, *op. cit.*

112. *Ibid.*, p. 30.

113. *Ibid.*, p. 28.

114. See Chapter Three, p. 40.

115. Kohlberg, *op. cit.*

116. Catherine Morris Cox, *Genetic Studies of Genius: The Mental Traits of Three Hundred Geniuses*, Vol. II, Stanford University Press, 1926.

117. Charlotte Buhler, "The Human Course of Life in Its Goal Aspects," *Journal of Humanistic Psychology*, Spring 1964, pp. 1–18.

118. Appendix to the *Discourse on the Origin of Inequality*, *op. cit.*, p. 239.

119. Hadley Cantril, *The Why of Man's Experience*, Macmillan, New York, 1950, p. 159.

Chapter five

120. Plato's *Republic*, Books 8–9.

121. Ernest Becker, *Beyond Alienation*, Braziller, New York, 1967, p. 187.

122. Robert S. Lynd, *Knowledge for What?*, Princeton University Press, Princeton, N.J., 1969.

123. Scott Paradise, "The Vandal Ideology," *The Nation*, December 29, 1969, pp. 730 and 732.

124. Wesley Mitchell is cited in Lynd, *op. cit.*, pp. 32–33.

125. The quotation is the opening of Harold D. Lasswell's *Politics: Who Gets What, When, How*, McGraw Hill, Whittlesey House, New York, 1936.

126. David Easton published *The Political System* in 1953 and *A Framework for Political Analysis* in 1965. The definition of the function of the political system as "the authoritative allocation of values" appears in both. See the latter work, Prentice-Hall, Englewood Cliffs, N.J., 1965, pp. 50–57.

127. D. A. Strickland, L. L. Wade, and R. E. Johnston, *A Primer of Political Analysis*, Markham, Chicago, 1968, p. 38.

128. For information about what is sometimes done in scientific experiments, see Catherine Roberts, *The Scientific Conscience*, Braziller, New York, 1967, and Theodore Roszak, *The Making of a Counter Culture*, Doubleday & Co., Anchor Books, New York, 1969, pp. 269–89.

129. Julius Seeman, "Deception in Psychological Research," in *American Psychologist*, Vol. 24, No. 11, November 1969, pp. 1025–28.

130. Quoted in Joseph Wood Krutch, *Thoreau*, William Sloane Associates, 1948, p. 173.

131. This phrase is the title of Chapter VII in Roszak, *The Making of a Counter Culture, op. cit.*

132. Mumford, *The Transformations of Man, op. cit.*, p. 116.

133. Quoted by Mumford in *The Condition of Man*, Harcourt, Brace, Jovanovich, Inc., New York, 1944, p. 417.

134. Maslow, *Toward a Psychology of Being, op. cit.*, p. 189.

135. Charles A. Reich, *The Greening of America*, Random House, New York, 1970, pp. 354, 358.

136. Joseph Wood Krutch, *Thoreau, op. cit.* p. 256.

Chapter six

137. Abraham H. Maslow and John Honigmann, "Synergy: Some Notes of Ruth Benedict," *American Anthropologist*, Vol. 72, No. 2, April 1970, pp. 320–33.

138. On this point, see Leslie Lipson, *The Democratic Civilization*, Oxford University Press, New York, 1964, p. 47.

139. R. H. Tawney, *Religion and the Rise of Capitalism*, Harcourt, Brace, New York, 1926.

140. Mumford, *The Condition of Man, op. cit.*, p. 253.

141. Arthur E. Morgan, *The Small Community*, Harper & Bros, New York, 1942.

142. This discussion is based on J. B. Bury, *The Idea of Progress*, Dover Publications, New York, 1955, pp. 206–15.

143. *Ibid.*, p. 208.

144. See Chapter One, p. 13 and note 26.

145. This quotation from Emerson, and those that follow, are taken from Brooks Atkinson (ed.), *The Complete Essays and Other Writings of Ralph Waldo Emerson, op. cit.*; Frederic I. Carpenter, *Emerson Handbook*, Hendrick's House, New York, 1953; *Encyclopaedia Britannica*, 1969 edition, Vol. VIII, p. 332–34; Lewis Mumford, *The Golden Day*, W. W. Norton & Co., New York, 1926; Ralph L. Rusk, *Life of Ralph Waldo Emerson*, Charles Scribner's Sons, New York, 1949; Louis Untermeyer, *Lives of the Poets*, Simon & Schuster, New York, 1959, pp. 541–44; Stephen E. Whicher, *Freedom and Fate: An Inner Life of Ralph Waldo Emerson*, University of Pennsylvania Press, Philadelphia, 1953.

146. The material on Thoreau is based on Van Wyck Brooks, "Thoreau," Leo Hamalian and Edmond L. Volpe (eds.), *Pulitzer Prize Reader*, Popular Library, New York, 1961, pp. 384–406; *Encyclopaedia Britannica*, 1969 edition, Vol. XXI, pp. 1073–75; Joseph Wood Krutch, *Thoreau, op. cit.*; Lewis Mumford, *The Golden Day, op. cit.*

147. J. S. Mill, *On Liberty*, Chapter III.

148. J. S. Mill, *Representative Government*, Chapter VIII.

149. Buber in Read, *op. cit.*, p. 287.

150. Rousseau, *Social Contract*, Book II, Chapter V.

151. Eight governments abstained, however, including the U.S.S.R., other Communist governments of eastern Europe, Saudi Arabia, and South Africa.

152. From *The Universal Declaration of Human Rights: A Standard of Achievement*, United Nations, 1958, p. 10, our italics. Mrs. Eleanor Roosevelt, chairman of the Commission on Human Rights which drafted the Declaration, said that it "may well become the international Magna Carta of all men everywhere."

153. *The Impact of the Universal Declaration of Human Rights*, United Nations, New York, 1951, p. 8.

154. *The Universal Declaration*, *op. cit.*, p. 10.

155. *International Conference on Human Rights*, Teheran, 1968, United Nations, New York, 1968, p. 3. The quotation is from Clause 2.

156. *Ibid.*

157. Catholic comes from the Greek *kath'holou*, meaning universal.

158. In *Pacem in Terris*.

159. *Ibid.*

160. Morgan, *The Small Community*, *op. cit.*, p. 92.

161. Morgan, *ibid.*, p. 116.

162. D. H. Lawrence, *Phoenix*, London, 1936, p. 382.

163. Aldous Huxley, *The Perennial Philosophy*, World Publishing Co., Meridian Books, Cleveland, 1962, p. 96.

164. Robert S. Morison, "The Need for New Types of Excellence," *Daedalus*, Vol. 90, Fall 1961, p. 37.

165. Buber, *I and Thou*, 2nd ed., Scribner's, New York, 1958, p. 11.

166. Buber quoted in Roszak, *The Making of a Counter Culture*, *op. cit.*, p. 201.

167. Mumford, *The Transformations of Man*, *op. cit.*, p. 173.

168. Reich, *The Greening of America*, *op. cit.*, p. 4.

169. John Rader Platt, "The Coming Generation of Genius," *Horizon*, March 1962, pp. 70–75.

170. Dennis Gabor, *Inventing the Future*, Knopf, New York, 1964.

Chapter seven

171. Shakespeare, *King Lear*, IV.1.38–39.

172. See Aldous Huxley, *The Perennial Philosophy*, *op. cit.*

173. Quoted by D. J. R. Bruckner, "U.S. Melancoly—So Deep It's 'National

Disease',” from *Los Angeles Times,* and *Washington Post* Service, reprinted in the *Oregonian,* May 28, 1970.

174. Read, *op. cit.,* p. 284.

175. Charles S. Silberman, *Crisis in the Classroom,* Random House, New York, 1969.

176. The cognitive domain has been studied by Benjamin S. Bloom and David Krathwohl. See Benjamin S. Bloom, (ed.), *Taxonomy of Educational Objectives,* Longmans, Green, New York, 1956.

177. Among these may be included Kenneth Boulding, Teilhard de Chardin, Aldous Huxley, Archibald MacLeish, Lewis Mumford, Gunnar Myrdal, Catherine Roberts, Anne Roe, and Arnold Toynbee.

178. Martin Scheerer, “Cognitive Theory,” *Handbook of Social Psychology,* Vol. I, Addison-Wesley, Cambridge, Mass., 1954.

179. *King Lear,* III.4.106.

180. Lewis Mumford, *The Story of Utopias,* Viking Press, Compass Books, New York, 1962, p. 277.

181. Polanyi, *Personal Knowledge, op. cit.*

182. Edith Sitwell, “Experiment in Poetry,” in *Tradition and Experiment in Present-Day Literature,* Oxford University Press, London, 1929, p. 97.

183. See Chapter Five, pp. 80 ff.

184. Paul Wienpahl, “Spiritual Values in a Scientific Age,” *Manas,* April 27, 1966, p. 2.

185. Article on “The Quest for Synthesis,” *Manas,* November 17, 1965, p. 2.

186. See the article on “Teaching and Healing,” *Manas,* March 25, 1970, p. 1.

187. Werner Heisenberg, *Physics and Philosophy,* Harper & Bros., New York, 1958, p. 58.

188. Michael Polanyi, *Science, Faith and Society: A Searching Examination of the Meaning and Nature of Scientific Inquiry,* University of Chicago Press, Phoenix Books, 1964.

189. Gerald Holton, “The Roots of Complementarity,” *Daedalus,* Vol. 99, No. 4, Fall, 1970, pp. 1015–1055.

190. Excellent evaluations of these new departures include Ernest Becker, *Beyond Alienation,* Braziller, New York, 1967; and Floyd Matson, *The Broken Image, op. cit.*

191. Willis W. Harman, “The Nature of Our Changing Society: Implications for Schools,” ERIC Clearinghouse on Educational Administration, Eugene, Oregon, October 1969.

192. Erich Fromm, *The Art of Loving, op. cit.,* p. 63.

193. Leo Tolstoy, *What Is Art?* Bobbs-Merrill, Indianapolis, 1960.

194. Alvin Toffler, “Future Shock,” *Horizon,* Vol. XII, No. 2, Spring, pp. 82–89.

195. Edith Sitwell, “The Poet’s Vision,” in Richard Thruelsen and John Kobler,

(eds.), *Adventures of the Mind*, Random House, Vintage Books, New York, 1958, p. 117.

196. Percy B. Shelley, *The Selected Poetry and Prose of Shelley*, The New American Library, Signet Classics, New York, 1966, p. 448.

197. "Is 'Art' the Remedy?" *Manas*, January 1, 1969, p. 7.

198. Simone Weil, *The Need for Roots*, Putnam, New York, 1942.

199. Quoted by Sitwell, "The Poet's Vision," *op. cit.*, p. 116.

200. Lucian Price, *Dialogues with Alfred North Whitehead*, Little, Brown & Co., Boston, 1954.

201. Sitwell, "The Poet's Vision," *op. cit.*, p. 116.

202. "Crossing the Line," *Manas*, August 14, 1968, p. 7.

203. Herbert Read, "Art and Life," in *Adventures of the Mind, op. cit.*, p. 158.

204. Read, "Art and Life," *op. cit.*, p. 169.

205. Irwin Edman, *Arts and the Man*, W. W. Norton, New York, 1939, p. 18.

206. Dante, quoted from the end of *The Divine Comedy*.

207. Michael Polanyi, *The Tacit Dimension*, Doubleday, New York, 1966.

208. Albert Camus, *The Myth of Sisyphus*, Random House, Vintage Books, New York, 1955, p. 137.

209. Herbert Read, *The Origins of Form in Art*, Horizon Press, New York, 1965, p. 187. The quotation that Read uses is from Martin Heidegger, *An Introduction to Metaphysics*, Yale University Press, New Haven, 1959, p. 45.

210. This poetry ranges from the writings of William Blake to Walt Whitman, from Dylan Thomas to Ferlinghetti and Gary Snyder. A careful study of this genre of writing may be found in James E. Miller, Jr., *et al.*, *Start with the Sun: Studies of Cosmic Consciousness*, University of Nebraska Press, Lincoln, 1960.

211. See Carl Rogers and Barry Stevens, *Person to Person—The Problem of Being Human*, Real People Press, Lafayette, California, 1967; and also Sidney M. Jourard, *The Transparent Self*, D. Van Nostrand Co., Princeton, N. J., 1964.

212. Pitirim A. Sorokin, *The Ways and Power of Love, op. cit.*

213. Maslow, *Toward a Psychology of Being*, 2nd ed., *op. cit.* p. 191.

214. Henry Anderson used these words in correspondence with the authors. For his views on this point, see p. 37.

215. Kenneth Clark, "Intelligence, the University and Society," in *The American Scholar*, Winter 1966–67, pp. 23–32; René Spitz, "Anaclitic Depression. An Inquiry into the Genesis of Psychiatric Conditions in Early Childhood: II," in Anna Freud, *et al.* (eds.), *The Psychoanalytic Study of the Child*, International Universities Press, New York, 1946; see also Margaretha Ribble, *The Rights of Infants*, Columbia University Press, New York, 1943.

216. C. G. Jung, *The Undiscovered Self*, Mentor Books, New York, 1957, p. 58.

217. Mumford, *The Condition of Man, op. cit.*, p. 54.

218. Maslow, *Toward a Psychology of Being*, 2nd ed. Chapter 6, "Cognition of Being in the Peak Experiences."

219. Fromm, *The Art of Loving*, op. cit.

220. The quotations from Buber are taken from Read's translation of a lecture which Buber gave on the concept of creativity at Heidelberg in 1925. See Read's *Education through Art*, op. cit., pp. 286–94.

221. Rogers and Stevens, op. cit., p. 47.

222. Jahoda, op. cit.

223. Fromm, *The Art of Loving*, op. cit., p. 49.

224. *Ibid.*

225. Sorokin, op. cit., p. 11.

226. Buber in Read, op. cit., p. 288.

227. Sorokin, op. cit., p. 200.

228. Polanyi in Roberts, op. cit., pp. 30–31.

229. Sorokin, op. cit., p. 253.

230. Sorokin, op. cit., pp. 243–45.

231. Joan Baez, interview in *Playboy*, July 1970, pp. 53–64.

232. Data from a word-frequency study done in 1960 by R. C. Johnson, C. S. Thomson and G. L. Frincke, psychologists at San Jose State College.

233. This was the consensus of honors students at Michigan State University, expressed to Elizabeth Monroe Drews during the period 1957–66.

234. Thomas Flemming, "The Organization S.O.B.," *Cosmopolitan*, September 1969. His account of "the corporate tough guy" is drawn from data and descriptions by W. Lloyd Warner and James Abegglen in their book *Big Business Leaders in America*, Harper & Bros., New York, 1955.

235. James Thurber, "The Tigress and Her Mate," *A Thurber Carnival*, Harper & Bros., New York, 1945.

236. Ian D. Suttie develops these concepts in *Origins of Love and Hate*, London, 1935.

237. Fromm, *The Art of Loving*, op. cit., pp. 39–40.

238. Sorokin, op. cit., p. 79.

239. This statement of Anton Julius Carlson was quoted in Robert Coughlan, "Now Within Sight: 100-Year Lifetime," *Life*, April 25, 1955, pp. 156–73.

240. Maslow, "Some Frontier problems in Mental Health," *Personality Theory and Counseling Practice*, University of Florida, Gainesville, January 1961, p. 4.

241. Sorokin, op. cit., p. 60.

242. Fromm, *Revolution of Hope*, Harper and Row, New York, 1968, p. 90.

243. Hui Neng, quoted by Aldous Huxley, *The Perennial Philosophy*, op. cit., p. 139.

244. St. Paul, *Epistle to the Romans*, 12:02.

245. Shakespeare, *Julius Caesar*, I.2.139–40.

246. Mumford, *A Story of Utopias, op. cit.*, p. 4.

247. On the fear of the unknown, see Milton Rokeach, *The Open and Closed Mind*, Basic Books, New York, 1960, and also Maslow, *Toward a Psychology of Being*, 2nd ed., *op. cit.* Chapter V. "The Need to Know and the Fear of Knowing," pp. 60–70. On the development of unused ability, consult Herbert Otto, *Explorations in Human Potentialities*, Charles C. Thomas, Springfield, Ill., 1965; and Paul Goodman, *The Present Moment in Education, op. cit.*

248. Julian Huxley, Galton Lecture, 1962, cited by Roberts, *op. cit.*, p. 19.

249. N. J. Berrill, *Man's Emerging Mind*, Dodd, Mead and Co., New York, 1955.

250. Aldous Huxley, *The Perennial Philosophy, op. cit.*, p. 14.

251. *Ibid.*, p. 92.

252. Mumford, *The Condition of Man, op. cit.*, p. 55.

Chapter eight

253. Mumford, *The Story of Utopias, op. cit.*, p. 281.

254. John R. Platt, "The Step to Man," *Science*, Vol. 149, August 6, 1965, p. 612.

255. Aldous Huxley, *The Perennial Philosophy, op. cit.*, p. 3.

256. Rollo May, *Love and Will*, W. W. Norton, New York, 1969, p. 306.

257. Francis Thompson, from "The Mistress of Vision."

258. Watson Thomson, *Turning Into Tomorrow*, Philosophical Library, New York, 1966, p. 57.

259. See Beverly Gross, "In a World of Analysis," a review of Grover Smith, (ed.), *Letters of Aldous Huxley*, Harper and Row, New York, 1969, in *The Nation*, June 8, 1970, pp. 693–95. Huxley made this comment in a letter where he was referring to his dystopic vision of the kind of society toward which we seemed to be heading. The details of the controlling system were made compellingly vivid in his novel, *Brave New World*, and in a series of essays, *Brave New World Revisited*, written thirty-two years later.

260. Bucke, *Cosmic Consciousness, op. cit.*

261. De Chardin, *The Phenomenon of Man, op. cit.*

262. Platt, *The Step to Man*, John Wylie, New York, 1966.

263. Huxley, *The Perennial Philosophy, op. cit.*, p. 92.

264. Quoted in *Manas*, "The Great Restoration," April 22, 1970, p. 3.

Index

Bible, 42, 55, 93, 98, 124, 126, 139, 142, 144; Book of Genesis, 51; Gospel, 76; Sermon on the Mount, 126
Bill of Rights, 105, 124
Biological Imperative, 49, 143, 152
Biology, 33ff, 43, 89, 162
Blacks, 22
Blake, William, 14, 43–44, 52, 55, 66, 78, 156 n.27, 165 n.210
Bloom, Benjamin S., 163 n.176
Bodhissatva, 15
Bohr, Niels, 28, 128, 157 n.44
Boulding, Kenneth, 89, 145, 164 n.177
Brahms, Johannes, 55
Breughel, the Younger, 134
Brook Farm, 108
Brooks, Van Wyck, 162 n.146
Brown, John, 96
Bruckner, D. J. R., 163 n.173
Bruner, Jerome, 67, 161 n.108
Bryant, William Cullen, 51, 159 n.79
Buber, Martin, 100, 114, 122, 136, 138ff, 163 n.149, n.165, n.166, 165 n.220, n.226
Bucke, Richard, 64, 66, 154, 160 n.107, 167 n.260
Buddhism, 43, 55, 72, 85
Buhler, Charlotte, 68, 161 n.117
Burckhardt, Jakob, 94; and *The Civilization of the Renaissance in Italy*, 94
Burke, Edmund, 78
Bury, J. B., 162 n.142, n.143

Calvin, Jean, 6, 181 n.10
Camus, Albert, 55, 132, 135, 150, 160 n.85, 165 n.208; and *The Stranger*, 150
Cantril, Hadley, 69, 161 n.119
Capitalism, 77, 80–81, 85, 93, 100
Carlson, Anton Julius, 143, 166 n.239
Carlyle, Thomas, 20, 78, 157 n.31
Carpenter, Frederic I., 162 n.145
Carr, Peter, 156 n.26
Carrighar, Sally, 49, 159 n.74
Carson, Rachel, 89
Catholicism, 85, 105, 125, 163 n.157
Cervantes, Miguel, 55
Chagall, Marc, 125
Change, 149; types of, 59–61, 99, 118

Chaos, 131, 132, 136, 151, 160
Chardin, Teilhard de, 63–64, 89, 154, 160 n.102, 164 n.177
Chekhov, Anton, 55
Child, Irvin L., 57, 186 n.86
Child, Lydia Maria, 50
Children, 23, 37, 44, 53, 62ff, 82, 100, 111, 117, 120, 131, 137 143, 149, 167
China, 11, 64, 154
Choice, 1–4, 12, 17, 22, 33, 36, 57, 65, 93, 107, 119, 153
Chomsky, Noam, 40, 67, 89, 90
Christianity, 11, 43, 55, 74–76, 85, 93, 129, 143
Church, the, 25, 75
Ciardi, John, 30
Civil disobedience, 11, 147
Civil rights movement, 117
Civilization, 7, 38, 44, 45–46, 53, 55, 58, 68, 98, 102, 105, 122, 134, 147; Asian, 54; Western, 25, 67
Clark, Kenneth, 136, 165 n.215
Coleman, James, 36, 158 n.51
Coles, Robert, 181 n.10
Colwell, Thomas B., 30, 157 n.47
Communication, 40, 107, 120, 123, 128, 132, 151; nonverbal, 37, 43
Communion, 52, 122, 139, 146
Communism, 85, 100, 163 n.151
Community, 3, 13, 15, 26–27, 36, 55, 64, 71–73, 74, 92, 94, 101, 116, 122, 126, 145, 147, 150, 153
Compassion, 114, 141, 143, 150
Competition, 7, 24, 43, 44, 48, 101, 122, 143, 146, 151
Complementarity principle, 28, 53, 123, 128, 139, 151, 157 n.44
Complexity, 28, 60–61, 67, 128, 131, 147, 150
Comte, Auguste, 87
Concord, Massachusetts, 96ff
Conditioning, 8, 10, 23, 86, 139; operant, 9, 82, 152
Condorcet, Marquis de, 13, 94, 99, 101, 156 n.23
Conformity, 26, 64–66, 77, 86, 99, 101, 111, 116, 144, 153
Confucianism, 43, 85, 159
Confucius, 30
Conscience, 10, 25, 65–66, 77, 90, 100, 114

Kropotkin, Peter, 48; and *Mutual Aid*, 48

Krutch, Joseph Wood, 38, 99, 158 n.55, 162 n.130, n.136, n.146

Kuh, Katherine, 56, 116, 161

Laing, Ronald D., 43, 89, 159 n.66

LaMettrie, J. O. de, 127, 147; and *Man a Machine*, 127

Laney, James T., 157 n.42

Language, 1, 40, 55, 67; origin of, 40, 62

Lasswell, Harold D., 81, 161 n.125

Laubach, Frank, 39

Law, 26, 75, 95, 104; canon, 126; of Nature, 149; and order, 78; supremacy of, 26

Lawrence, D. H., 113, 163 n.162

Learning, 65, 107, 133, 137, 149

Leibniz, G. W. von, 25

Leonardo da Vinci, 93

Levellers, 77

Lévi-Strauss, Claude, 40, 89

Liberation, 15, 37, 54, 78, 90, 115, 126, 145

Liberty. *See* Freedom

Lincoln, Abraham, 41

Linguistics, 21, 40, 124, 150

Lipson, Leslie, 159 n.76, 162 n.138

Liu, Sidney, 155 n.19

Locke, John, 9–11, 72, 78, 93, 97, 152, 155 n.17; and *Essay on the Human Understanding*, 9

Loevinger, Jane, 62ff, 160 n.93, 161 n.110

Lorenz, Konrad, 46; and *On Aggression*, 46

Love, 1–3, 4, 8, 12, 34, 36, 44, 45, 52, 57, 73, 75, 87, 91, 102, 108, 114, 116, 120ff, 124, 129, 134, 136–146, 148, 150, 151

Lowie, Robert, 45, 159 n.71

Lucretius, 51; and *On the Nature of Things*, 51

Luther, Martin, 93

Lynd, Robert S., 79, 161 n.122, n.124

MacLeish, Archibald, 164 n.177

McLuhan, Marshall, 30, 157 n.46

Machiavelli, Niccolo, 6, 8, 76, 93, 100, 116, 155 n.9; and *The Prince*, 6, 76

Machines. *See* Technology

Magna Carta, 22, 103, 163 n.152

Man: Faustian, 175; Hobbesian, 6–7, 46, 81, 152; Lockean, 10–11, 177; Promethean, 175; universal, 64, 154

Mankind: common genetic heritage of, 34; study of, 4, 79; unity of, 27, 39, 42, 52, 101ff, 108, 117, 150, 154

Mao Tse-tung, 11

Markham, Edwin, 52

Marx, Karl, 78, 100

Maslow, Abraham H., 2, 8, 15–16, 34, 36, 43–44, 51, 62ff, 89–90, 91, 137, 143, 148, 153, 158 n.1, n.2, n.16, 160 n.64, n.98, 162 n.134, 165 n.213, n.218, 166 n.240, n.247; and *Toward a Psychology of Being*, 15

Materialism, 25, 51, 54, 64, 80, 86, 93, 97, 122

Matson, Floyd, 155 n.18, 157 n.44, 164 n.190

May, Rollo, 150, 167 n.256

Mayflower Compact, 108, 151

Mead, Margaret, 89

Meaning, 2, 4, 22, 40, 52, 85, 119, 131, 136, 145, 150

Media, 9, 30, 38, 77, 135, 141

Medici, 77

Mennonites, 108

Metaphysics, 19, 74, 99, 123, 127

Michael, Donald, 89, 150

Michelangelo, Buonarroti, 132

Middle Ages, 71, 76, 92, 126

Military, 76, 77, 80, 113

Mill, John S., 22, 96, 99, 101, 162 n.147, n.148; and *Liberty*, 99; and *Subjection of Women*, 100

Miller, James E., 165 n.210

Mills, C. Wright, 89

Milton, John, 22

Mitchell, Wesley, 81, 161 n.124

Mithraism, 11

Mohammedanism, 42, 55, 85

Montagu, Ashley, 44, 159 n.69

Moore, Ruth, 157 n.44

Morality, 13, 26, 38, 43, 44, 58, 65, 88, 95, 97; corruption of, 54. *See also* Ethics

Morgan, Arthur E., 94, 108, 162 n.141, 163 n.160, n.161; and *The Small Community*, 108

Morison, Robert S., 114, 163 n.164
Morris, Desmond, 46; and *The Naked Ape*, 46
Morris, William, 13
Mozart, Wolfgang, 24
Muir, John, 52, 159 n.80, n.81
Mumford, Lewis, 25, 63–64, 67, 87, 89–90, 94, 114, 124, 144, 146, 149, 157 n.40, 160 n.100, 162 n.132–134, n.140, n.145–146, 163 n.167, n.177, n.180; 165 n.217, 166 n.246, n.252, 167 n.253
Mussolini, Benito, 81
Mutual Adoption Club (M.A.C.), 111
Myrdal, Alva and Gunnar, 89, 164 n.177
Mysticism, 42, 55
Mystics, 28, 89, 92, 96, 98, 124, 145; Eastern, 30, 98, 145

Nation-state, 76, 100, 102, 113, 136
Nationalism, 77, 104, 163
Nature, 3, 26, 36, 47–58, 77, 87–88, 97, 117, 121, 128ff, 139, 145, 151; balance of, 30
Needs, 33ff, 91; anthropological basis of, 33–40; biological basis of, 33–40; inner, 92; physical, 33; psychological basis of, 23, 33–40; spiritual, 33, 34; universal, 40, 150
Neill, A. S., 44, 159 n.68; and *Summerhill*, 44, 159
Neo-Platonists, 124
Neurosis, 82, 134, 137, 150
New Harmony, Indiana, 108
Newton, Isaac, 9, 29, 97, 125, 126, 127
Nightingale, Florence, 13, 146

Objectivity, 2, 18–21, 38, 73, 79ff, 83ff, 127, 131, 138, 150
Oligarchy, 25, 74, 117
Oneida Community, 108
Opportunism, 64ff, 68, 116
Optimism, 12–13, 89, 94, 98, 143
Order, 8, 26, 40, 72–73, 76, 96, 121, 134
Organism, 10, 33–36, 129, 137
Organization, 86, 101, 114, 142, 147
Orient, 14, 89, 98
Orwell, George, 10, 101; and *1984*, 10, 101

Otto, Herbert, 166 n.247
Overpopulation, 27, 49, 113

Paideusis, 108
Paine, Thomas, 13, 25, 156 n.25
Paleontology, 89
Papacy, 76–77, 93, 105, 126
Paradise, Scott, 80, 161 n.123
Parochialism, 27, 113, 126
Parrington, Vernon L., 156 n.25
Pasternak, Boris, 7; and *Doctor Zhivago*, 7
Paul, Saint, 166 n.244
Pavlov, Ivan, 9, 82
Peace, 42, 46–49, 52, 75, 81, 94, 106, 110, 130, 140, 142, 154
Peace Corps, 117
Peck, Robert, 62ff, 160 n.96
Peden, William, 96, 150 n.26
Pericles, 93
Perry, Ralph Barton, 41, 157 n.30, n.36, 158 n.62
Persia, 11, 50
Pessimism, 5–7, 145, 152
Philosopher-king (guardian), 3, 15, 74, 130, 158
Philosophy, 41–42, 71–72, 88, 120, 124, 130, 135, 136; of art, 55; of education, 22; existentialist, 17, 21; of history, 89; of life, 1, 3; moral, 41–42, 97, 103; natural, 126; political, 6; social, 72, 73ff, 78, 88–90, 93ff, 101, 127, 148
Physics, 28, 97, 123, 126, 128, 137, 150
Physiology, 9, 128
Piaget, Jean, 67
Plato, 3, 6–7, 15, 23, 55, 72, 74, 92, 97, 116, 119, 122, 124, 133, 155 n.4, 161 n.120 and the *Republic*, 72, 74, 124, 130
Platt, John, 89, 117, 149, 154, 163 n.169, 167 n.254, n.261
Pluralism, 26, 29
Polanyi, Michael, 3, 63–64, 84, 89, 124, 128, 135, 140, 155 n.3, 160 n.103, 164 n.181, 165 n.188, n.207, 166 n.228; and *Personal Knowledge*, 84
Political science, 80–89, 157, 161 n.126
Politics, 77ff. *See also* Government
Pollution. *See* Ecology

Pope, Alexander, 4
Positivism, 21, 157 n.37
Potentialities, 14ff, 33–36, 38, 41, 61ff,
82, 91, 95ff, 99, 113, 123, 129, 134,
136, 144–145, 149, 154; physical
outer limits of, 34
Poverty, 22, 47, 54, 75–76, 80, 87–88,
114, 117, 126, 142
Power, 6, 7–8, 11, 17, 26, 51, 63, 72–
78, 81, 85, 89, 93, 101, 127, 137,
152; seekers of, 10, 101, 116, 122,
126; structure of, 75, 85ff, 88, 127
Price, Lucian, 165 n.200
Price, Willard, 159 n.70
Priestley, J. B., 116
Priorities, 1, 4, 33, 60, 93, 100, 116,
120, 121, 146
Progress, 13, 27, 30, 94ff, 113ff
Protestant Ethic, 24, 93
Protestantism, 85
Psychoanalysis, 2, 8, 89
Psychology, 6, 11, 20, 33–38, 62, 74–
79, 81–83, 89, 125, 137ff, 142; exis-
tential, 28; experimental, 38, 79,
82–84; Gestalt, 20; humanistic, 8,
28, 68, 82; science, of, 29; and sen-
sation, 97; social, 80, 83
Psychopathology, 43, 63, 68

Quakers, 25, 77, 154
Quantification, 38, 59–60, 79–81, 137

Race relations, 94–95, 105, 114, 146
Radicalism, 78, 95–96, 128, 143, 148
Raphael, 132
Read, Herbert, 36, 45, 55–58, 133ff,
158 n.52, 160 n.90, 162 n.149, 163
n.174, 165 n.203, n.209, n.220, n.226
Reality, 23–27, 28, 41, 54, 84, 89, 98,
113, 124, 129, 149
Reason, 13, 29, 42, 74–75, 100, 115,
120, 126, 136
Reciprocity, 138ff
Redfield, Robert, 89
Reductionism, 29, 38, 84, 125, 128
Reformation, 76, 92
Reformers, social, 13, 97, 98
Reich, Charles A., 16, 24, 77, 89–90,
115, 162 n.135, 163 n.168; and The
Greening of America, 16
Relativism, 17, 27–31, 38, 42

Religion, 11–12, 14, 40–42, 46, 67, 72,
74, 87, 97, 103, 105, 117, 120, 126,
133
Religious denominations, 66–67, 114
Rembrandt, 56
Renaissance, 55, 76–77, 92, 94, 116,
129
Research, empirical, 74, 78–79, 83–84,
87–88, 90
Responsibility, 2, 17, 112, 132, 138
Reston, James, 109
Revolution, 6, 16, 100, 133, 142; Amer-
ican, 13, 94; Bolshevik, 7; French,
13, 68, 78, 94; of values, 16, 76ff,
102; of youth, 27
Ribble, Margaretha, 165 n.215
Rich, John Martin, 44, 159 n.67
Riesman, David, 64, 100
Riis, Jacob, 13
Roberts, Catherine, 89–90, 114, 160
n.106, 161 n.128, 164 n.177, 166
n.228, 167 n.248
Roe, Anne, 121, 164 n.177
Rogers, Carl, 63–64, 89, 139, 160 n.99,
165 n.211, n.221
Rokeach, Milton, 166 n.247
Roles, Social, 84, 90, 125, 136, 152
Romans, the, 58, 75, 93, 126
Romantic movement, 51ff, 88–90
Roosevelt, Eleanor, 146, 163 n.152
Roszak, Theodore, 16, 84, 89, 161
n.131, 163 n.166; and The Making
of a Counter Culture, 16
Rousseau, Jean Jacques, 13, 37, 42, 53,
68, 72, 78, 93, 101, 145, 156 n.24,
162 n.118, n.150
Rusk, Ralph L., 162 n.145
Ruskin, John, 52, 159 n.81
Russell, Bertrand, 38, 115, 158 n.56
Russia: czarist, 50, 55; the Soviet
Union, 7, 163 n.151

Sabi, 54
Sanger, Margaret, 13
Sartre, Jean Paul, 17
Scheerer, Martin, 164 n.178
Schiller, Friedrich von, 120
Schools, 23, 36, 43–44, 65, 86, 97,
108, 137ff, 146, 158 n.51. See also
Education

Schopenhauer, Arthur, 8, 155 n.13; and the *Parable of the Porcupines*, 8
Schrag, Peter, 157 n.43
Schweitzer, Albert, 13
Science, 21, 28–30, 77, 78–79, 84–88, 100, 122, 125ff, 132, 136, 137–138, 147, 154; humanistic, 124; physical, 85, 89, 154; psychology of, 29; social, 19, 30, 38, 41, 43–44, 65, 73, 78–88
Scientific method, 79ff, 125, 137
Seeman, Julius, 82–83, 161 n.129
Self, 90, 92, 101, 123, 136: actualization of, 15–16, 44, 57, 62ff, 68, 72, 113ff, 131, 138, 143, 148, 153ff; aggrandizement of, 93, 146; awareness of, 1ff, 5, 17, 36, 65, 92, 119, 139, 141, 144
Self-fulfilling prophecy, 72
Senses, the, 4, 9, 13–14, 35, 52, 57
Sex, 34, 39, 66, 114
Shakers, 77
Shakespeare, William, 1, 51, 55, 123, 132, 144, 159 n.77, 163 n.171, n.179, 166 n.245; *As You Like It*, 51; *Hamlet*, 124, 135; *The Tempest*, 51
Shaw, G. B., 78, 149
Shelley, Percy B., 55, 57, 132, 134–135, 160 n.88, 164 n.196
Silberman, Charles, 120, 163 n.175
Simplicity, 51, 54, 60, 76, 145, 151
Sitwell, Edith, 124, 132ff, 164 n.182, n.195, n.199, n.201
Skinner, B. F., 10, 82, 152; and *Walden Two*, 10, 152
Slavery, 24, 72, 75, 94, 97, 104
Smith, Grover, 167 n.259
Snyder, Gary, 165 n.210
Social class, 22, 66–67, 72
Social contract, 93
Social Security, 105
Socialism, 100
Socialization, 17, 36, 43, 45
Society, 3, 11, 13, 16, 24, 26, 36, 43, 45, 53, 57, 91, 94, 95, 99, 101, 134, 136, 139, 151; origin of, 40; sickness of, 151. *See also* Utopia
Sociology, 38, 83, 89, 142
Socrates, 4, 20, 64, 75, 129, 135
Sophocles, 129

Sorokin, Pitirim, 89, 114, 136ff, 150, 152, 165 n.212, 166 n.225, n.227, n.229, n.230, n.238, n.241
Soul, 11–12, 86, 93, 114, 121, 130, 141
Specialists, 89–90
Spencer, Herbert, 46
Spinoza, Baruch, 30
Spirit, 15, 30, 36, 43, 51, 74–76, 78, 82, 85, 87, 120, 126, 132, 153, 154
Spitz, Rene, 137, 153, 165 n.215
Spontaneity, 26, 52, 72, 116, 134, 139, 153
Stalin, Joseph, 9, 81, 101, 152
Status, 51, 67, 73–74, 93, 143, 159
Stevens, Barry, 165 n.211, n.221
Stoicism, 74, 93
Strickland, D. A., 161 n.127
Students, 23, 86–87, 143, 150; in college, 83, 111, 142; in high school, 36, 39, 43, 110
Subjectivity, 4, 16, 18–22, 62, 73, 79ff, 83ff, 91, 106, 127
Suttie, Ian D., 14, 142, 165 n.236
Synergy, 16, 92, 113, 136
Synthesis. *See* Unity

Tabula rasa, 9, 10–11
Taoism, 129
Tawney, R. H., 94, 162 n.139
Tea Ceremony, 54, 58
Teachers, 39, 58, 65, 87, 132, 135, 137ff, 143, 147
Teaching, 57, 88, 100, 103, 120, 151
Technology, 16, 27, 45, 77, 87, 97, 100, 113, 126–129, 147, 149
Tennyson, Alfred, 52
Theobald, Robert, 89
Theology, 6, 11–12, 20, 93, 105, 126; the New, 26
Thomas, Dylan, 165 n.210
Thompson, Francis, 150, 167 n.257
Thomson, C. S., 166 n.232
Thomson, Watson, 151, 167 n.258
Thoreau, Henry David, 25, 35, 55, 78, 84, 89, 90, 96, 97, 101, 145, 162 n.130, n.136, n.146; and *Walden*, 98
Thruelsen, Richard, 164 n.195
Thucydides, 6–7, 129, 155 n.70
Thurber, James, 142, 166 n.235
Tocqueville, Alexis de, 118
Toffler, Alvin, 131, 164 n.194

Tolstoy, Leo, 13, 55, 130, 134, 164 n.193; and *War & Peace*, 124
Toscanini, Arturo, 24
Totalitarianism, 101, 152
Toynbee, Arnold, 12, 89, 164 n.177
Tradition, 54, 59, 64, 73, 106, 143
Transcendentalism, 14–15, 38, 89, 97ff, 124
Trust, 12, 107, 108, 113, 150–151
Truth (Eternal Verities), 1ff, 13, 18, 20, 34, 36, 38, 54, 68, 73, 77, 91, 107, 120–129, 135–137, 143, 148, 150, 151
Twain, Mark, 44
Tyranny, 74, 94, 112

Ulich, Robert, 121
Unconscious, 1, 4, 14, 20, 29, 119, 143; collective, 41, 45, 154
UNICEF, 39
Uniqueness, 25, 26, 36, 72, 104, 116, 123, 139, 153
United Nations, 103ff
United States, 13–14, 23–25, 45, 53, 80, 103
Unity, 42, 72, 76, 150–151, 153
Universal Declaration of Human Rights, 103ff, 115, 163 n.152
Universality, 13, 22, 25, 27–28, 64, 66, 74–75, 101–113, 118, 123, 131, 148, 153
Universities (Academia), 9, 22, 86–87, 98, 122, 132, 142–143
Untermeyer, Louis, 155 n.5
Utopia (good society), 4, 10, 26, 41, 72, 78, 89, 94, 149, 153, 157

Values, 17, 26, 33, 134, 135, 147; hierarchy of, 1ff, 27, 53, 59–71, 102ff, 117, 120, 148; higher, 2, 16, 27, 36, 38–39, 43, 57, 60, 72, 87–88, 91, 102ff, 113, 115, 117, 119–146; lower, 36, 60, 72–73, 77, 80ff, 84, 93, 143; reinterpretations of, 36; as related to the object valued, 3, 18–22; as related to the person valuing, 3, 18–22; and relation to actual and ideal, 18ff, 41ff, 113; as relative and universal, 27–31; revolution of, 16, 76, 92, 94, 102, 108, 115, 148; universal foundations of, 13, 33–58

Vietnam, 85, 87, 124, 148
Violence, 38, 43, 94, 100, 113, 122, 130, 134, 137, 147
Virgil, 159 n.82
Virtue, 53, 74, 95, 100, 119, 151, 160 n.106
Volpe, Edmond L., 162 n.146
Voltaire, 78
Vote, right to, 118

Wabi, 54
Wade, L. L., 161 n.127
Waldenses, 76, 77, 108
War, 4, 7, 43, 46, 49, 72, 75, 81, 87, 94, 100, 113, 117, 122, 134, 142, 152; the American Civil, 24; the English Civil, 77, 113; as just, 75, 106; the Spanish Civil, 101
Ward, Barbara, 89
Warner, W. Lloyd, 166 n.234
Washington, George, 25
Watson, J. B., 9, 82
Wealth, 54, 73, 75, 81, 93, 113, 117
Webster, Daniel, 97
Weil, Simone, 132, 164 n.198
Westermarck, Edward W., 158 n.57
Whicher, Stephen E., 162 n.145
Whitehead, Alfred, 89, 165 n.200
Whitman, Walt, 25, 52, 95, 133, 146, 151, 165 n.210
Wienpahl, Paul, 126, 164 n.184
Wiese, Leopold von, 157 n.34
Wilde, Oscar, 69; and *The Picture of Dorian Gray*, 68
Wilder, Thornton, 136; and *The Bridge of San Luis Rey*, 136
Wisdom, 74, 79, 83, 151
Women, 22, 35, 94, 95, 97, 100, 104ff, 110, 117, 146, 154
Wordsworth, William, 37, 51, 78, 121, 133, 158 n.53; and "The World," 51

Yeats, William, 57
Youth, 27, 43, 62, 86–90, 102, 117, 122, 134, 136, 140, 142, 147
Yusutani-Roshi, 31

Zen Buddhism, 31, 54
Zoroaster, 11
Zwingli, Ulrich, 93